NOAH STRYCKER is a photographer
Birding magazine. Called a 'travel
on-board ornithologist and guide on polar expeditions, and has
worked on field research projects in Amazonian Ecuador, Costa
Rica and the Australian Kimberley, among other places. He has
written for a wide variety of bird magazines and is the author of
Among Penguins, *The Magic & Mystery of Birds* and *Birds of the Photo Ark*.

Praise for Noah Strycker:

'This beautifully written book is a treasure trove of information
on the avian world, from the life-long relationship of the
albatross to the remarkable memory of the nutcracker'
BBC Countryfile

'[This book] turns a shrewd, comparative eye on a succession
of bird families to explore what [Strycker] calls their "human"
characteristics ... This is an engaging work which illuminates
something profound about all life, including our own' *Economist*

'[Strycker] explains in wonderful stories that penguins are afraid
of the dark (leopard seals wait in black waters to gobble them up)
and that albatrosses truly love one another (mating for life and
using each other's breasts as pillows) ... As Strycker writes, "by
studying birds, we ultimately learn about ourselves"' *New York Times
Book Review*

'Mr Strycker has the ability to write about the worlds of man and
fowl without simplifying either ... He thinks like a biologist but
writes like a poet, and one of the small pleasures of [this book]
is watching him distil empirical research into lyrical imagery ...
Part the palm fronds behind his sentences, and you can almost
see the British naturalist and broadcaster David Attenborough
standing there in a pith helmet, smiling with amused approval at
Mr Strycker's off-centre sensibility' *Wall Street Journal*

BIRDING WITHOUT BORDERS

AN OBSESSION, A QUEST
AND THE BIGGEST YEAR IN THE WORLD

NOAH STRYCKER

FOREWORD BY KENN KAUFMAN

SOUVENIR
PRESS

This paperback edition first published in 2021

First published in Great Britain in 2018 by
Souvenir Press
an imprint of Profile Books Ltd
29 Cloth Fair
London
EC1A 7JQ
www.profilebooks.com

First published in the United States of America by
Houghton Mifflin Harcourt Publishing Company.

Published by arrangement with Houghton Mifflin Harcourt Publishing Company.

Book design by Eugenie Delaney

1 3 5 7 9 10 8 6 4 2

Printed and bound in Great Britain by
CPI Group (UK) Ltd, Croydon, CR0 4YY

A CIP catalogue record for this book is available from the British Library.

ISBN 978 1 80081 011 2
eISBN 978 0 28564 416 8

CONTENTS

FOREWORD

B irds are real. If I had to justify extreme birding, that would be my first defense. Even as we dash around in a mad quest for the biggest list of bird sightings, we're keenly attuned to reality—not just the birds but also geography, weather patterns, forest types, tide schedules, and myriad other factors, because everything in nature is connected. Other people may take up hobbies to escape reality, but birding has the opposite draw. It's a deep dive into the real world.

A year is also a real thing—one orbit around the sun—and yearlong birding efforts are the epitome of extreme birding. The first "Big Years" were done in the 1890s by Lynds Jones and W. L. Dawson in Lorain County, Ohio, cooperating and competing to run up their county tallies. By the 1930s, a few birders were competing for the biggest annual list for all of North America north of Mexico. The popularity of the pursuit has been creeping up ever since, and so have the totals produced. Recent North American Big Year champs have pushed the theoretical maximum and cratered their bank accounts by flying back and forth across the continent, chasing every rarity that strayed within our boundaries.

I myself did a Big Year as a teenager in the 1970s, on a very modest budget, but the restriction of boundaries rankled. I took time out for three trips into Mexico that year, even though birds south of the border wouldn't "count." The allure of tropical diversity was irresistible. Even then, the wide world of variety beckoned more than the idea of birding within borders.

Peter Alden, a pioneer leader of international birding tours, had ticked more than 2,000 species globally during 1968. We all thought that was cool, but in that era, no one seriously thought about topping that score. World birding was hard. Thousands of tropical bird species had never been illustrated at all, and good field guides existed only for North America, Europe, and South Africa. Bird-finding publications were almost unheard-of outside the United States. Birding tours still took in relatively few destinations. For my friends and me, an overseas birding trip involved weeks of preparation, and often more research afterward to figure out what we'd seen. As rewarding as these trips were, no one wanted to cram too many into a single year.

In the few decades since that time, world birding has gone through two major revolutions, utterly changing the game.

The first big change, gradual but massive, has been the information explosion. Today, every known bird species has been superbly illustrated. Practically anywhere on Earth, we can choose among multiple bird ID guides. Thousands of "mystery birds" are now less mysterious, their secrets revealed. Excellent sound recordings make all the difference in finding elusive targets, especially in dense tropical haunts. At one time, if you wanted to see a Zigzag Heron, for example, you wandered in the Amazon Basin for a year and prayed for a miracle. Now that its voice and precise habitats are known, this weird little wader isn't hard to find.

An even bigger change is the emergence of a worldwide community. Not long ago birding was a lopsided pursuit, popular in a few English-speaking countries, plus northern Europe and Japan. Between these silos of activity, communication was limited. The rise of the Internet changed that. Listservs brought about instant communication among the continents. Social media like Facebook even broke the language barrier with the sharing of bird photos and automated translation. At the same time, local birding communities have sprung up in most nations. In the past, if you wanted advice on birding Colombia, you sought out North Americans or Europeans who had been there. Today that country has a thriving birding scene, and Colombian experts know their own avifauna better than any outsider. Knowledge is now decentralized. And since birders everywhere tend to be open and sharing, travelers now have vastly more potential sources of help.

For birding the world, the biggest driver of change is eBird, the massive online database of bird sightings. Launched in 2002, eBird was limited to North America at first, going global in 2010. Its acceptance and growth worldwide have been phenomenal, and it utterly changes how we perceive the potential in distant lands. Once, when reading about Blyth's Hawk-Eagle in the Malay Peninsula and Indonesia, it would have seemed impossibly remote. Now a few clicks into eBird will display half a dozen sites where the species has been seen within the last month, and we can check how consistent it is at those sites and who the local observers are. It's no exaggeration to say that eBird has become the global hub for active birders.

As world birding has evolved, the global year list record has pushed upward. The American ornithologist James Clements ran up a total over 3,600 in 1989—just before the Internet became a factor. An intrepid British couple, Alan Davies and Ruth Miller, surpassed 4,300 species in 2008—just before eBird went global. The time was ripe for someone to push past 5,000, recording more than half the world's birds in a single year. The previous champs—Alden, Clements, Davies, and Miller—have all been friends of mine, and I watched with keen interest to see who would be next.

We could not have hoped for a better contender than Noah Strycker. This brilliant young man was already a veteran of detailed field research, already renowned for writing about birds with depth and grace; no one could dismiss him as "just a lister." In one carefully planned, continuous sprint around the globe, he shattered previous records. He also made a point of going native and connecting with local experts everywhere. The result is a thoughtful, vivid portrait of the world's birds and birders.

At this moment in history, it's easier than ever to see birds worldwide . . . and all over the planet, birds face unprecedented perils. A pessimist might say we're in the sweet spot between accessibility and extinction. I don't see it that way. Noah Strycker turned up plenty of birds on his grand tour, but more important, he met people in every land who care passionately about those birds and who will fight for their survival. Everything in nature is connected, and as the birders of the world become more connected also, the reality of the future looks brighter already.

—Kenn Kaufman
March 2017

1

End of the World

ON NEW YEAR'S DAY, superstitious birdwatchers like to say, the very first bird you see is an omen for the future. This is a twist on the traditional Chinese zodiac — which assigns each year to an animal, like the Year of the Dragon, or Rat — and it's amazingly reliable. One year, I woke up on January 1, glanced outside, and saw a Black-capped Chickadee, a nice, friendly creature that everybody likes. That was a fantastic year. The next New Year, my first bird was a European Starling, a despised North American invader that poops on parked cars and habitually kills baby bluebirds just because it can. Compared to the Year of the Chickadee, the Year of the Starling was pretty much a write-off.

So it was with some anxiety that on January 1, 2015, I looked around to see which bird would set the tone for the next 365 days. I already knew this would be no ordinary year: I'd just quit my only regular job, broken up with my girlfriend, spent most of my savings, and then, cramming all my possessions into a small backpack, made my way literally to the end of the Earth. Now, at the stroke of midnight, on top of a Russian ship in the frozen reaches of Antarctica, with a bottle of champagne in both hands and binoculars dangling around my neck, I was in a hot tub with a Scottish historian, a penguin researcher, and a geologist. What bird could possibly tell where all of this was heading?

With any luck, it would be a penguin. I'd gone to great lengths to engineer this New Year celebration just so that, right after the obligatory countdown and toast, 2015 could be declared the Year of the Penguin — which, karmically speaking, couldn't possibly go wrong. In the previous week, I'd spent a lonely Christmas night on the floor of the Los Angeles airport, traveled from the United States to the southern tip of Argentina, caught this ship, sailed across the tumultuous Drake Passage, and positioned myself for this moment, this pivotal moment when fate would set in motion the biggest year of my life, and possibly of international birdwatching history.

The goal was simple: in the next twelve months, I hoped to see 5,000 species of birds — about half the birds on Earth — in the ultimate round-the-world journey. After leaving Antarctica, I'd spend the next four months in South America, then migrate north through Central America, the Caribbean, and Mexico, reaching the United States in May. If things went well, I'd fly over to Europe, do a big U-turn through Africa, bounce around the Middle East, zigzag across most of Asia, and island-hop Down Under to ring in the following New Year. While the Earth completed one full orbit of the sun, I would visit forty countries with no days off. Nobody had ever attempted such a trip, and bird-brained experts argued about whether it was even possible to spot 5,000 species in one calendar year. By the end, the journey would surpass even my own wildest dreams. But for now, all I knew was that the clock started ticking at midnight.

✦—✦—✦

The world's most frequent fliers don't have platinum status, free upgrades, or even passports. Every hour, millions of these undocumented immigrants pour across major political borders, and nobody thinks of building walls to keep them out. It would be impossible to anyway. Birds are true global citizens, free to come and go as they please.

A few years ago, two British scientists tackled the question of how many individual birds are living on Earth — a sort of global avian census — and calculated that, at any given moment, between 200 and 400 billion feathered friends share this planet with us. That works out to something like forty birds for every human, spread from here to Timbuktu. Birds occupy almost every conceivable niche of our world, from the wild Amazon in South America to the heart of the Bronx in New York City. Even places that seem lifeless lie within their reach: intrepid birds have been recorded at the South Pole, winging over the summit of Mount Everest, and soaring across the open ocean hundreds of miles from land. As of 2015, 10,365 bird species had been identified on planet Earth, a number that only begins to hint at their sheer diversity. The smallest, the Bee Hummingbird of Cuba, could perch comfortably on the toenail of the largest, the Ostrich.

Birding is a state of mind more than anything else, which makes it hard to define. Roger Tory Peterson, generally considered the father of modern birdwatching, once observed that birds are many things to many people: a science, an art, a sport. They can even, as Peterson's friend James Fisher added with a wink, "be a bore, if you are a bore." It's a tough activity to pigeonhole, though many have tried; birding is hunting, collecting, and gambling rolled into one. Nobody can decide whether birdwatching constitutes an addiction, a release, or just a game played by khaki-clad eco-nerds.

My own interest in birds was sparked innocently enough at the age of ten, when my fifth-grade teacher suction-cupped a clear plastic bird feeder to our classroom window. When I was twelve, my dad helped me build bluebird houses and took me to a bird-watching festival in eastern Oregon. Pretty soon I was dragging home rotting deer carcasses to attract and photograph Turkey Vultures, then deferring college to go study bird nests in Panama, then eschewing a nine-to-five job entirely, introducing myself as a "bird man" whenever anyone asked.

From the beginning, the pursuit gave me a sense of purpose. By watching the skies, I began to see the world in different and unfamiliar ways, letting curiosity lead me to new places. By my mid-twenties, I'd spent more than a year and a half occupying tents in various remote corners of the world, in between avian research projects and expeditions, and accepted that there was no going back. I also had a growing, slightly uneasy sense that even if I kept it up for the rest of my life, there were just too many birds and too little time.

The feeling of urgency seems to be everywhere. Psychologists call it FOMO (Fear Of Missing Out), conservationists call it habitat loss, and Hollywood directors call it The Apocalypse. In terms of connecting with the outdoors, we live at an interesting moment. A hundred years ago, people watched birds in hopes of finding new species, but the golden age of ornithological discovery has mostly passed; virtually all birds are now thoroughly, scientifically described, and tucked away as musty specimens in museum collections. Today, people are drawn to birding for the exact opposite reason: to rediscover and celebrate nature at a time when significant chunks of society rarely venture outdoors. It's poignant that, just as record numbers of people are paying attention, the birds themselves have never faced a more uncertain future. This planet is being cleared, flattened, tilled, drilled, paved, and developed at an unprecedented rate. What that means for birds, humans, and the rest of the world is unclear.

As easy as it is to get discouraged, birders are a particularly optimistic, action-oriented group. They know that you won't see much if you stare at the wall all day. They also know that some experiences can't be duplicated digitally. There is a special joy in watching an actual Scarlet Tanager instead of looking at a virtual red bird, however spectacular, on a phone screen. And by setting their sights on the freest creatures in the world, birders have a unique perspective about how their subjects stitch together even the farthest parts of our globe. Birds teach us that borders are just lines drawn on a map — a lesson we can all take to heart.

As my thirtieth birthday loomed, a grand plan emerged: to travel the planet, meet its most passionate birders, perhaps set a fun record, and take a unique snapshot of Earth, all in one swoop. I set out to see the world, one bird at a time.

About a hundred passengers and forty crew had converged for this Antarctic expedition, advertised as "New Year's Eve among Emperors and Kings" — a reference to the world's two largest penguin species. If you're going to see the world, you might as well start at the end of it, and Antarctica seemed like the perfect beginning for my yearlong journey.

As the official onboard ornithologist on this cruise for Canada-based One Ocean Expeditions, it was my job to point out the penguins and other wildlife until the ship returned to Argentina a week after the New Year. We traveled on the *Akademik Ioffe,* a Soviet-era vessel ostensibly built for oceanographic research but rumored to have once scouted American submarines during the Cold War. The trip's passenger manifest included doctors, lawyers, business people, technogeeks, and a variety of well-traveled and well-heeled types from South Africa, Australia, the United States, Europe, and other scattered countries, about a third of whom were bucket-listing their seventh continent. The interpretive staff, by contrast, were younger, free-spirited souls like me, many of them experts in their field, who could happily spend extended periods in remote parts of the world. This was my nineteenth polar expedition in the past three seasons, and it would be my last for a while.

As midnight arrived, strains of "Auld Lang Syne" wafted up from the ship's bar two decks below while four of us soaked in the hot tub outside. The geologist, a master's student named Casey from New York's Stony Brook University, shook up a champagne bottle and popped its cork like a starting gun. Its contents sprayed freezing foam on everything in sight.

"Happy New Year!" we shouted.

A few passengers emerged from the bar to take cell phone videos of us. Most people, which is to say normal people, don't celebrate New Year's by spraying champagne at each other in a hot tub in Antarctica. I gingerly shielded my binoculars. It was hard to focus because the whole world seemed to be rocking. Maybe it was the ship moving, or the champagne, or the general mayhem, or the hundred thousand miles of unknown lying ahead. But . . . no birds! Not one! Oh, I desperately wanted to find a penguin.

The Scottish historian, a red-haired doctoral candidate named Katie, caught my eye. "Well? Do you see anything?"

In the midnight sun, the view from the hot tub, strategically perched on the ship's upper deck, was unbeatable. Thousands of sculpted icebergs, glistening in shades of cobalt, sapphire, and steel, dotted the ocean as far as the eye could see, with a narrow line of dazzling glacier faces tracing the Antarctic mainland on one horizon. An artistic friend, inspired by a similar sight, once confided to me his idea to carve a few bergs to psych out passengers of passing ships: just imagine sailing past a mansion-sized block of ice in the Southern Ocean shaped like Mickey Mouse. But my friend was forced to admit that human creativity has nothing on the brute forces of nature, especially down here. An iceberg the length of a football field weighs a million tons, about the same as, oh, the annual wheat import in Ethiopia; and in the icy waters of the southern sea, I've seen bergs several miles wide. A few years ago, a chunk broke off the Ross Ice Shelf south of New Zealand that was bigger than the entire land surface of Jamaica; it drifted for several years, interfering with penguin and ship traffic alike. In this part of the world, the ice is likely tens of thousands of years old — perfect for an aged whiskey on the rocks — and the tip of an iceberg above water truly is only about a tenth of its full size. Watching icebergs is like watching birds: the more you think about them, the more insignificant you feel, and only gradually do you begin to sense how much lies beneath the surface.

The sun hung at a low angle, casting everything in its eerie glow. In the distance, I could see Trinity Island, a fifteen-mile-wide projection of ice and rock. It was too far away to make out the Gentoo and Chinstrap Penguins I knew were nesting in its sheltered harbor. Still, with a breeding colony so close, I figured I could spot one or two strays passing by. Penguins are perfectly capable of swimming hundreds of miles, and they like to rest on icebergs.

But . . . no penguins. On top of that, the hot tub was getting cold. Outdoor hot tubs are not really made for Antarctica, and this one couldn't keep up with the frigid temperature. If we didn't hit the sauna soon, the four of us would turn into icicles.

"Do goosebumps count as a bird?" asked Nicole, the young penguin researcher, and no one answered.

In the austral summer, when phytoplankton flourishes in twenty-four-hour sunlight, the Southern Ocean is perhaps the single most productive place for life on Earth — and yet there were no signs of life at all, not a single whale spout or seal. In the so-called land of penguins, where was a penguin when you really — *really* — wanted one?

Someone said: "You're the worst birder in the world! How are you ever going to reach five thousand if you can't even find number one?"

Casey got out, then Katie. Water sloshed over the side of the hot tub and froze on the metal deck. Nicole took off. Which left just me, the self-described bird man, sitting alone in a half-filled, half-frozen hot tub in Antarctica near one o'clock in the morning, with zero penguins in sight.

What could I do? Birds are fickle souls. I picked up a towel, followed the others inside to warm up, and abandoned my carefully scripted plan to spot my first bird of the year from a hot tub at the end of the world. All around me in the narrow corridors, people straggled toward their cabins. With the ship's lights dimmed for dusk, a uniformed Russian officer soberly patrolled the bridge, and a Canadian bartender mopped up in the bar. Throughout the ship, people tucked into their bunks, and things settled down after a long and lively evening. Adventures awaited after breakfast — namely, a visit to a large penguin colony, where I was guaranteed to see thousands of the tuxedoed birds on the first day of the New Year.

But I was just too keyed up to sleep. After most everyone had ambled off to bed, I pulled on two layers of long underwear, wool socks, a pair of ski pants, a fleece sweater, a waterproof down jacket, a fleece neck warmer, a pair of insulated waterproof gloves, a wool toque, a pair of fleece-lined waterproof boots, and binoculars, and headed out. This time, instead of staking out the upper deck, with its expansive view, I made my way to the very back of the ship, where I could look down its roiling wake. Wedged on the stern deck between a winch, a large crane, coils of rope, and several inflatable Zodiac boats lashed in place, I stood sheltered from the wind by a metal dumpster storing all of the expedition's garbage, and leaned on the rail.

This was my favorite spot on the ship. Personal space is scarce on a 383-foot-long vessel occupied by 140 people, so I retreated here whenever I wanted a moment alone. Nobody ever went behind the dumpster. Plus, some species of seabirds like to follow vessels, and I often saw birds coursing the wake, occasionally hanging in the breeze almost close enough to touch. None was visible now, but at least this was a nice vantage point.

Could I really spend a whole year birding the world without burning out? I wasn't sure. From now until the end of December, I planned to do nothing else. I would be so focused that I'd skip some of the great wonders of the world — Machu Picchu in Peru and the Taj Mahal in India — just for a couple more hours of stalking birds in the nearby forests. Was that gauche? My friends love to poke fun at me for constantly chasing birds, and I admit that "taking time off" is kind of a foreign concept. But 365 days of predawn awakenings, total strangers, and nonstop, grueling travel would test the limits, sort of like a drug addict doing nothing but cocaine for a year. If it didn't completely break me down, it would leave me high as a kite.

There was only one way to find out if I could hack it, and now I was committed.

My watch read 3 a.m. Suddenly, a hundred yards out, something flickered among the icebergs. In the low light, it almost escaped detection — appearing as a dark speck skimming the surface, zigzagging on broad tacks, gradually approaching the ship.

I knew what it was before even raising my binoculars. This bird flew on stiff wings, riding intricate wind currents deflected from waves; every now and then it flapped a series of snappy beats to change direction, but mostly it just glided on air. It was the length of a football and equally plump. Its head was matte black, contrasting with immaculately white underwings and belly, and its tail was dark. But the bird's most striking feature resolved when it banked toward me and swooped low, below eye level. The upper sides of its wings were spattered with frosty black and white blobs, a crisp vision of abstract expressionism.

Many people call this bird a "pintado," literally meaning painted, because of its splotchy appearance, but in proper English I had spotted a Cape Petrel, a relatively common Southern Ocean bird that nests on remote cliffs. Although Cape Petrels occasionally spew stomach oil from their beaks in fits of foul humor, they are admired and well liked by most people lucky enough to encounter them. This tough little seabird, trying to keep pace next to the ship at three in the morning, might not be a penguin, but it was perfect.

Petrels, in their infinite grace, are thought to be named for Saint Peter and his habit of walking on water. With a blessing like that, the Year of the Petrel was off to an auspicious start.

2

The DSP

ACCORDING TO THE American Birding Association's Recording Rules and Interpretations, a bird must be "alive, wild, and unrestrained" for official consideration on a birder's list of sightings, be it a world list, year list, world year list, life list, national list, state list, county list, month list, yard list, feeder list, birds-seen-while-driving list, or any other list. In other words, dead birds don't count, and you can't rack up exotic sightings in zoos and aviaries. Any bird "under the influence of captivity" is as illegal as can be.

The rulebook has a few more interesting tidbits. Webcams are a no-no for listing. Eggs don't count until they hatch, and chickens, as domestic animals, don't count at all (except the Red Junglefowl of Asia, the wild ancestor of barnyard stock). You can put an injured bird on your list, but not a perfectly healthy hybrid; to be countable, a bird must have the traits of one recognized species. Heard-only encounters are fine so long as recorders "assure themselves" that they aren't listening to someone else playing a tape from the bushes, a circumstance that happens surprisingly often.

Otherwise, keeping your list is up to you. Many people assume that birders must document every sighting as if collecting evidence for a court case, but that misses the spirit of the game. As a practical matter, it would be impossible to photograph them all — birds are often too far away or flitting too quickly to get a shot — and anyway, birding works on the honor system.

Not that a few con artists haven't tried to fudge the facts. Birders even have a name for them: fakers are called "stringers," and fabricating a sighting is "stringing." In one particularly egregious case several years ago in Australia, a birder announced his intention to see as many bird species as he could in one year in his home state. He spent the first few months notching up an impressive list of sightings, started a blog, and built a following. About halfway through the year, some local experts began to get suspicious; then, in a dramatic stroke, the guy was caught red-handed: he reported a frigatebird — a tropical species rarely seen in that part of Australia — and posted a photo of it flying against a blue sky. When it was pointed out that the weather on that day was cloudy, the man broke down and, in a long and cringing confession on the regional email list, admitted that he'd actually photographed the bird on a trip to Fiji. For such blatant stringing, the man was blacklisted by the birding community. As they say, you can lose your reputation only once.

But birding scandals are rarer than a Diademed Sandpiper-Plover. It's pretty easy to tell if someone's faking it, and there isn't much reason to make it up. Adding bogus birds to your list is like lying to your diary. What's the point?

Most birdwatching transgressions involve far more minor infractions. For everyday situations, the American Birding Association (ABA) maintains a "Code of Birding Ethics," which outlines respectable field behavior and follows common sense: don't stress birds; give nests enough space; respect private property; keep your bird feeders clean. The ethical code advises birders to "be especially helpful to beginning birders" and "support the protection of important bird habitat."

The rules leave a few gray areas. For instance, if you snap a photo and later discover a bird in the image that you hadn't noticed before, can you count it? If you are standing near an international border and spot a bird on the other side, can you record it for a country in which you have never set foot? Situations like these come up constantly, and not all birders give the same answers.

Also, just because the rules allow certain birds, it doesn't mean you have to count them. Some birders count only self-found sightings, omitting any bird first identified by someone else. Others, who designate themselves NIB — "no introduced birds" — try to keep their lists pure by excluding non-native species. The thorny subject of introduced birds involves various official committees and whole swaths of gray areas. In short, established feral species are legitimate, but the word "established" has inspired heated debates. Even the term "native" is problematic.

The most contentious part of the ABA's recording rules is Rule 4, Section B, which allows birds that are heard but not seen. Despite this rule, many birdwatchers note only visual sightings and pay little attention to sounds beyond the most familiar ones. Jotting down heard-only birds can seem almost like cheating; some species that are phenomenally difficult to spot, like cryptic owls and skulking rails, are relatively easy to hear. Few people would dispute that the distant call note of a Stygian Owl is somehow less satisfying than having the bird itself stare back at you. And yet some bird species have such distinctive calls, why wouldn't you count them, even if you didn't see them?

For my Big Year, I decided to tally both seen and heard birds. The previous single-year world record had counted heard-onlys, so

I'd be applying the same standard. Also, it's better for the birds: listening has less impact than playing recordings, trampling through a bird's territory, or flushing it in a desperate attempt to get a visual. Many species are best appreciated by their sound, anyway; one might argue that you haven't really experienced a Screaming Piha until you've heard one. Vocalizations are as reliable as visual field marks, and lots of drab-looking species have lovely, distinctive songs. In wide-open environments, such as Antarctica and the Chilean Andes, it's easy to see almost everything; but in places such as the Amazon, where birds hide in thick jungles, the soundscape becomes more important. By the end of this year, I would identify about 5.5 percent of the birds I encountered — one in eighteen species — by ear alone.

Although hard to believe in this globalized age, there is no single, agreed-upon checklist of all the bird species on Earth. Instead, we have competing interpretations: the Americans versus the rest of the world. In the United States, most birders use the Clements Checklist, which is periodically updated by experts at Cornell University and which recognized 10,365 living bird species while I traveled in 2015. In Europe and other parts of the world, birders tend to rely instead on the International Ornithological Congress (IOC), a progressive committee that acknowledged 10,612 species in 2015. Some countries, notably the Netherlands and Brazil, have adopted their own, even more liberal checklists. The trouble is, birds don't always fit into neat boxes, and many so-called species blur into each other. On top of that, scientists lately have been re-evaluating birds around the world with DNA evidence, and in the past couple of decades they've proposed thousands of "splits" — dividing one species into two or more — narrowing our definition of what a species should be.

You need rules to play the game, and for my year I adopted the Clements Checklist — the American standard. It helped that eBird, the app I use to keep track of sightings, is based on the same checklist. Along the way, I would keep notes on subspecies, too, so that it would be possible to dynamically adjust the tally. These days, a list of birds is more software than hardware, and keeping it up to date presents an unending task.

A week after the New Year, high in the Andes Mountains of central Chile, I went looking for an oddball animal called the Diademed Sandpiper-Plover. Two local birders from Santiago, Fred Homer and Fernando Díaz Segovia, came along to help with the search, and the three of us were switchbacking up a magnificent Andean valley at dawn.

Months before, I had asked a friend in Arizona if he knew any good birders in Chile, and he referred me to Fabrice Schmitt, a Frenchman who, after taking a teaching sabbatical in South America, had been inspired to move to Santiago to lead birdwatching tours. Fabrice replied right away with regrets that he would be on a trip to Antarctica when I arrived in Chile — but kindly put me in touch with Fred, who thoroughly embraced the mission.

"We'll meet you at the airport and dash off to hunt the birds," Fred emailed, "and then we'll rush you back with tires smoking."

Fred then called Fernando, a young Chilean biologist, who picked us up at oh-dark-thirty that morning. And that's how it went: a friend of a friend of a friend of a friend — someone I had neither met nor even corresponded with — was now taking me to see one of the world's most enigmatic birds in the world's longest mountain range.

The Diademed Sandpiper-Plover, or DSP as birders call it, is a peculiar creature, found only at high elevations in Chile, Argentina, Bolivia, and Peru. It is a shorebird that doesn't live on the shore, apparently related to plovers but with a profile more like a sandpiper (hence the hyphenation). No other bird looks much like it: the DSP, about the size and shape of a dinner roll, has a dumpy body, fat yellow legs, a droopy beak, a deep reddish collar, finely barred underparts, and an upturned white mark behind each eye — the "diademed" part — that gives it a quizzical expression. The bird looks like it doesn't mind being stared at but wonders why anyone would bother.

You won't stumble across one by accident unless you spend a lot of your spare time stumbling around desolate Andean bogs, as Fernando does. For the past few years, Fernando has been tracking sandpiper-plovers, trying to coax out their secrets. As part of a research project, he surveys likely looking habitat; for some reason, the DSP is reliably found in some bogs but not in others that look just the same, and nobody has figured out why the bird is so darned picky. Fernando also captures each bird so that he can mark it with color bands, which help identify individuals from a distance. Keeping track of all these little sandpiper-plovers is like following a soap opera, but maybe the data will unlock some of their mysteries.

Fernando drove us in his freshly washed SUV up a dusty gravel road that emerged above tree line and continued, hacked into a cliff, up a steep-sided valley. The route was so narrow in places that only one vehicle could pass. When we nosed around a corner to find an oncoming car, Fernando painstakingly reversed along the sheer drop to a slightly wider spot, then folded in his side mirrors to allow the other vehicle to squeeze by.

While we climbed, I sat in the passenger seat, my thoughts drifting back over the previous week. After kicking off the New Year with champagne and a Cape Petrel off the Antarctic Peninsula, the year's bird count had progressed slowly. I quickly ran out of Antarctic birds to see, and on January 3 — just the third day of the year — recorded no new species at all, notching my first zero day practically out of the starting gate. The pace picked up with albatrosses and other seabirds on the Drake Passage, followed by a fantastic morning at a colony of charismatic Southern Rockhopper Penguins in the Falkland Islands. But by the time our ship returned to port in Ushuaia, the world's southernmost city at the southern tip of Argentina, I'd recorded only 53 species of birds in the first seven days of the year. With the need to average 13.7 new species each day — about one bird for every daylight hour — to break 5,000 by the end of December, my score was already lagging.

A full week in Antarctica wasn't exactly strategic, because there aren't enough species on the whole continent to keep up this average. If I had scheduled the same time somewhere in the tropics, I would have seen two or three hundred birds by now, well ahead of the target pace — starting my marathon with a sprint rather than a lope. But then I would have missed the world's coldest and driest and windiest continent, with its massive colonies of Adélie and Chinstrap Penguins, spouting humpback and minke whales, impossibly blue icebergs, and unparalleled ice cap. To me, Antarctica underlined, from the beginning, that this year was not just about numbers. Any global journey that skipped Antarctica wouldn't be as cool.

Still, as our ship neared the dock, I was ready to pick up the pace. I felt light and happy. Everything lay before me — uncertainty, opportunity, and a limitless planet of birds and birders. The sun bathed the world in a hopeful light, and I had the exhilarating feeling that I was exactly where I should be, doing exactly what I should be doing. There would be challenges, but I was eager to explore. I was a little apprehensive, too. I couldn't help wondering whether the local birder I planned to meet would actually show up.

In the few hours after the ship docked in Ushuaia, before flying on to Santiago, Chile, I hoped to track down some Patagonian bird specialties in nearby Tierra del Fuego National Park. An Argentine birder named Esteban Daniels, whom I had contacted months before, had agreed to help — but now that the day had come, would he remember me? I said a round of hurried goodbyes to the ship's staff and crew, grabbed my backpack, and walked down the gangway onto Ushuaia's industrial dock. There, outside the pier's security checkpoint, awaited Esteban and a friend, a keen photographer named Rogelio "Roger" Espinosa. I was ecstatic to see them — and relieved. Over the next couple of hours, Esteban, Roger, and I stopped by the local landfill, then made our way to the park, where we found my most-wished-for bird species of the day: a pair of red, black, and white Magellanic Woodpeckers, the largest woodpecker in South America. We clocked thirty-seven new bird species — bringing my year total so far to ninety-one — before heading to the local airport in midafternoon.

After a quick flight to Santiago, I sped through immigration, skipped the baggage claim, and headed straight for Exit 3, where Fred Homer, exactly as planned, awaited in a green hat. So far, so good! Fred and I crashed at his house in Santiago, where Fernando picked us up in the early morning hours, and now the three of us were hot on the trail of the Diademed Sandpiper-Plover.

The road continued to climb, skirting around a shallow reservoir in a broad valley of rock and dirt, which was birdless except for a lone Andean Gull flying in lazy circles.

"A couple years ago I came down here," Fred said, "and, maybe three hundred meters from this spot, saw something on the road ahead. As I got closer, I realized that it was the rear axle of a lorry, implanted into the road surface. When you looked around, there were bits of lorry all over the place. I guess it went off the edge above and just fell to pieces."

All plant life ceased as we ascended into the upper El Yeso Valley, flanked on both sides by chiseled peaks in ochre and umber. The sky up here looked polarized, like the deep blue you see through sunglasses. Snowfields clung to the mountaintops, almost at eye level, and I could see bluish, crevasse-wrinkled glaciers hanging from steep slopes above us. Every so often we passed a *Vía de Evacuación* ("Evacuation Route") sign, illustrated with a friendly stick-figure image of mother and child walking in front of an exploding volcano.

Fernando turned at an unmarked junction at about 10,000 feet and followed a side track until it petered out into boulders. The three of us jumped out and walked a little farther to the only speck of green in this valley, where a snowmelt stream fanned into a bog of squishy, carpetlike vegetation.

This, Fernando said, is the realm of the DSP, and he led us straight into the bog. Surrounded by the stark landscape, Fernando looked the part of a rugged biologist: checked shirt, khaki cap, glacier goggles with mountaineering flaps around the temples, work pants, low-slung binoculars, and a slightly unkempt beard. He wasn't much older than me and shared the same bent for fieldwork in remote places. He had quit working as a landscaper to focus full-time on bird research. Now he was in his element, scanning for movement.

Fred wandered behind us in the sunshine, smiling, enjoying just being out here. A few years ago he'd moved to Chile, after retiring in Britain from a career in financial services, and set up a bird-touring business as an excuse to spend more time watching birds. He wore a gray vest with lots of pockets over a collared T-shirt, aviator shades, and a wide-brimmed hat with braided leather accents; his trimmed beard was 25 percent pepper, 75 percent salt.

Halfway across the bog, I almost stepped on our target. Fernando pointed toward my feet, and I looked down just in time to see the Diademed Sandpiper-Plover staring up with beady-eyed curiosity. It was completely unafraid as an animal a hundred times its size blundered toward it, and I wondered if this behavior might have something to do with the bird's low population. Nobody knows how many sandpiper-plovers are out there, but the best guess is about 2,000 individuals scattered over an area half the length of South America. They don't have many predators, at least not in human form, and part of the DSP's charisma is its totally blasé attitude — as if it knowingly trusts you.

An impossibly cute, fuzzy chick emerged from behind some nearby rocks and the two birds slowly waddled off together, probing for bugs with their droopy beaks. They wore matching green and red plastic bands on their right legs, and the adult had a red and yellow combination on the left. Fernando noted down the colors, adding another data point to the DSP project — and I chalked up species number 123 for my Big Year list.

The sandpiper-plover is listed as near-threatened because of its vulnerable populations. In the high Andes, insidious effects such as atmospheric disturbances and climate change could have serious impacts on the DSP's habitat, but it's hard to tell without enough data. Fernando hopes that more surveys will document patterns, which might eventually help with conservation efforts. We lingered until lengthening shadows reminded us that, despite its star status, the Diademed Sandpiper-Plover still counted as only one species.

"It would be pointless to bust a gut to see Chile's most rare and beautiful bird," Fred said, "if you could, in the same duration, find ten locally common and ugly ones that you weren't going to see elsewhere."

He was right, of course. When all birds are created equal, no bird is worth a significant amount of time. It's an age-old tradeoff: you can go narrow and deep, or broad and shallow, but you can't focus in all dimensions at once. I took one last look at the Diademed Sandpiper-Plover, and we drove off to see how many ugly Chilean birds we could find.

Later that evening, Fred and I sat on his backyard patio in a leafy Santiago suburb. Fred served up a bowl of pasta and a fresh salad and poured us each a glass of red wine. The last rays of daylight caught the upper branches of a tree next to the patio. January is the hottest month of the year in Chile, and the afternoon's warmth hung in the air. We'd returned before dark to try for a Rufous-tailed Plantcutter that sometimes visited Fred's yard at dusk. As we waited, it was nice to sit back after a long day in the mountains.

"I'm not really a very serious birder," Fred said, "in the sense that I like watching birds, but I don't particularly care what the species is. I just like watching them. And, of course — today was a prime example — it takes you to some very nice places."

That's what I like about it, too. Birding is always an adventure, and it gives you focus when you travel, instead of staring yourself glassy-eyed at too many tourist attractions. Fred got hooked on birds from one of his sons, who caught an interest at a young age. Although his son's attention passed on to other things, Fred has been addicted to birds ever since.

"It was like a relay race — he handed off the baton, and I kept going," he said.

The sun was setting, its last rays of light fading from the trees. The evening air felt cool and refreshing after the blasting mountain sunshine and dust. Just then, from the corner of my eye, I caught a movement.

"Could you hand me my binocs?" I asked.

Even in the dim light, there was no mistaking this bird: chestnut crown and breast, dark cheeks, white wing bar, serrated beak. A plantcutter! The plump little bird, named for its tendency to shred and eat leaves, had returned at dusk, as Fred predicted. It peered down at us for a minute before fluttering off to its nighttime roost. I was delighted with its brief visit, the sensation heightened by sharing it with Fred, a person I barely knew but with whom I already felt a deep connection. We thoroughly embraced the moment.

"A nice glass of wine, a delicious dinner," Fred said. "Now *this* is birding!"

3

Cerro Negro

WHEN I TOUCHED DOWN in northwest Argentina, the arrivals area of the tiny airport in Jujuy (pronounced hoo-HOO-ey) was deserted. I wandered around for a few minutes with my backpack and binoculars, then walked outside and sat down on the curb to wait. The few other passengers from my flight drifted into cars and drove away, leaving me in an empty parking lot. Would anybody pick me up?

I was a little fuzzy on the plan here. A birder named Freddy Burgos had invited me to visit his province for the next four days, but because Freddy speaks no English, I had been writing to him in my shaky Spanish. As far as I could tell, using Google Translate to fill in the gaps, Freddy had suggested a camping trip, but the details were vague. Maybe I hadn't quite grasped his instructions — was I supposed to meet him somewhere? I had no idea what he looked like, what his phone number was, or where he lived. At least the weather was nice, warm and sunny. Fluffy white clouds drifted over the airport's brick facade, perfect conditions for camping — if indeed that was the plan.

Sixteen days into the year, my bird list stood at more than 300 species, right on track for my 5,000-species goal. The pace had picked up dramatically when I arrived in central Argentina two days before. In Buenos Aires I met thirty-year-old birder Marcelo Gavensky and his friend Martin Farina, a twenty-eight-year-old dog trainer and paleontology student, and the three of us dashed up to the marshy cattle country of the Entre Ríos province, about 125 miles north of the city. On our first day, we found 146 species of birds — more than I'd seen in four full days in Chile — 108 of which were new.

The grasslands were fantastically productive. Between sips of hot *mate* (pronounced MAH-tay), Marcelo proudly told me about La Alianza de Pastizal, a conservation group that encourages ranch owners to practice sustainable grazing techniques. The idea is that, with the right methods, ranchers maximize profits with fewer cows, leaving a lighter impact on the landscape: certified, ecologically sensitive beef can be sold at a premium in Europe, and the Argentine market for it is growing. Shipping overseas isn't a perfect environmental solution, but well-managed *estancias* are the key to protecting habitat in this region, which has no designated parks or reserves. We saw dozens of prehistoric-looking Southern Screamers, a few towering Maguari Storks, and scattered, ridiculously pink Roseate Spoonbills in the fields. Around one corner, a five-foot-tall Greater Rhea stalked past — South America's answer to the ostrich.

After that quick visit, I crashed for a couple of hours on the floor of Marcelo's one-room apartment in Buenos Aires, with my feet in the kitchen and head wedged under the dining table, then bid *adiós* to central Argentina and caught an early flight to the northwest. Now, low on sleep, I sat outside the Jujuy airport and wondered what had happened to Freddy.

I was about to try sending him an email message from my phone when a small bird flitted around the departures area, and I jogged over to get a better view. It had a warm, brownish body, a gray face, and wings that flashed a rufous-red color in flight. This bird was definitely something new, but what? It behaved like a flycatcher, perching and sallying after insects, occasionally hovering to go after bugs in the corners of the eaves.

I closed the email browser and opened my phone's photo gallery. Packing a six-foot-high stack of heavy reference books around the world was out of the question, so before leaving home I had painstakingly scanned dozens of field guides and saved the images as digital files on my smartphone. In an album titled "Birds of Argentina," I swiped through illustrated plates to the flycatcher section and quickly found a match: the Cliff Flycatcher, a common inhabitant of South American forests and of airport lampposts, was bird number 338. This fine specimen was still flitting around twenty minutes later when a white pickup truck sped into the parking lot and stopped at the curb. Four young people jumped out, smiling and gesturing, and one of them extended a hand.

"Noah," he called, "*yo soy* Freddy!"

He was about my height, five nine, with a squat, stocky build. His hair was straight, jet black, and shaggily cut, long enough to cover his sideburns and the back of his neck, and he had a pointy beard at the tip of his chin, perfect for stroking — as I soon discovered he loved to do. He wore a military-green long-sleeved shirt, black field pants, and hiking boots. His most striking feature was his smile; he couldn't seem to wipe it off his face.

Freddy had brought along some friends, and as they clustered around, a lot of excited Spanish suddenly went flying past my ears. They were apologizing for the delay in picking me up, something to do with groceries and supplies, and introducing themselves all at once: Claudia Martin, José Segovia, and Fabri Gorleri. I was excessively glad to be among them, reassured by their welcoming kindness.

I threw my pack into the bed of the pickup, which was piled with enough gear to outfit a mountaineering expedition. What exactly had Freddy planned for the next four days? The five of us squeezed into the pickup's double cab and peeled out. As we left, the Cliff Flycatcher sallied in front of the windshield to pick off an insect, and from the back seat I pointed it out.

"*Sí, sí,*" said Freddy, who was simultaneously driving, navigating, and eyeing our gear to make sure nothing blew out. "*Hirundinea ferruginea.*"

It took a minute to realize that this was the bird's scientific name.

"Right, a Cliff Flycatcher!" I said. Everyone looked blank.

Of course, they had no reason to use English common names for birds. Most Latin American birders don't use Spanish common names either, because they aren't well standardized; instead, Spanish-speaking birders learn the international scientific classifications, a system in Latin that scientists around the world use to understand each other. This was going to make things interesting in the field, where new sightings come fast and furious.

Freddy drove straight out of town, and as civilization receded behind us, the truck turned off the highway and began to ascend a gravel road into lush east Andean foothills. Gradually I absorbed bits of information. Freddy worked as a biologist in Jujuy, and Claudia, his girlfriend, was a botanist with an interest in all natural things. José and Fabri were students at a university in eastern Argentina and had come more than six hundred miles by bus to join us. All four of them were between the ages of twenty-three and thirty-three and shared a love of birds and adventure.

When Freddy received my first email, he thought it would be a great opportunity to go camping at Cerro Negro, a seldom-visited mountain range with some special birds. No roads lead into the high elevations there, so we'd have to hike in more than ten miles and climb thousands of feet up a tortuous pack trail. Freddy had arranged for three mules to carry our stuff so that we could spend four nights in the Yungas cloud forest and Pastizal grassland above tree line, sleeping in tents. He said he'd packed plenty of food. We made a brief stop at a village to collect a driver who would return the pickup, and arrived at the trailhead in early afternoon. The road ended at a river that sliced through dense, green forest, with bare mountain peaks visible above the valley.

Sure enough, three mules — one white and two brown — appeared with their owner, a *campesino* in jeans and rubber boots, who lashed our bundles of gear to their saddles. I hoped Freddy had packed an extra sleeping bag, because my silk liner wouldn't keep me warm at high elevations. The mule team went ahead while Freddy, Claudia, José, Fabri, and I spent an hour meandering around the river. The sun had disappeared behind a layer of clouds, which was beginning to look worrisome, but birds kept popping into view.

"*Cypseloides rothschildi,*" Freddy shouted, and I saw a cigar-sized bird with sickle-shaped wings zooming overhead. It looked like a swift, and I scrolled through the field guide on my phone, trying to confirm the scientific name and its English equivalent. Aha! — Rothschild's Swift, a nice regional specialty and year bird number 342.

"*Psittacara mitratus,*" said Fabri, which I translated as a Mitred Parakeet, another new one.

"*Empidonomus varius!*" Claudia called out.

At the same time, José, looking in the opposite direction, announced, "*Progne elegans!*"

"*Sporophila lineola,*" Freddy added.

"Ay yay yay," I said.

I tried to ask them to wait while I looked up each bird name, but it was no use. Birds don't hang around to be identified, and I did my best to keep up with the onslaught of sightings, jotting down scientific names in a notebook for later reference when we hit a big canopy flock. Almost every bird in this part of Argentina was new to me, so I appreciated the help of these local experts in identifying fast-moving targets.

A pair of Torrent Ducks occupied this stretch of river, needing no translation. I'd seen one in Chile, so the species had already been counted for the year, but I paused for a few minutes to admire how they braved the whitewater. Like most ducks, the male had strikingly different plumage than the female — he was black and white with a red beak, while she was gray and orange — and they had long, slender bodies, streamlined for life in rushing water. The birds swam effortlessly through churning rapids, using their feet to propel against the flow. They appeared to be hunting for aquatic insects, inspecting the undersides of each boulder as they went.

I glanced up to see Freddy, pants rolled up past his knees and hiking boots swinging loosely around his neck, wade into the current. He turned and waved.

"Vámanos!"

Time to start hiking, or we'd arrive in camp after dark. The trail entered the forest on the far side of the river. There was no bridge.

Claudia, José, Fabri, and I removed our shoes and plunged in, taking extreme care with each step. The stream was ice cold, running fast, and up to my thighs. Knee-deep water moving at just four miles per hour can knock a person off balance, and one slip on these slick boulders might send any of us floating away down the river. I'd taken the precaution of lining my backpack with a water-proof garbage bag, but didn't relish the thought of getting soaked before even starting this hike.

The Torrent Ducks swam by as if paddling on a glassy pond,

then hauled out on a rock between two waterfalls and watched while we struggled across, dried our feet, and put our shoes back on.

Dark clouds were gathering in earnest now, obscuring the peaks in a heavy blanket. I remembered that I had landed in Jujuy only a few hours ago, and had been birding with Marcelo and Martin just yesterday afternoon, more than eight hundred miles away. The ranchlands of Buenos Aires already felt like a distant memory. Freddy pointed to a gap in the trees where the trail began to climb, and we walked into the forest just as the first rumble of thunder echoed down the valley.

Going solo and being alone are two very different things. I went solo in 2011 when I hiked the 2,650-mile Pacific Crest Trail, a backcountry route up the American West from Mexico to Canada, but I spent much of the time in company with other people. It would have been hard not to: hundreds of hikers attempt to walk the whole thing each year, and about 95 percent of them take the northerly option, as I did, to follow the progression of summer. During four "solo" months in the backcountry, I saw at least one other person every single day, and often hiked and camped with others.

On my Big Year, I was also going solo, in the sense that I planned the trip myself and that nobody traveled with me from place to place, but I didn't want to go birding alone. I made a point of seeking out bird-minded companions in each country I visited. Applying the lessons I'd learned from long-distance hiking, I went ultralight for the year, carrying only a forty-liter backpack with trail-tested gear and traveling in a steady progression to the seven continents, with no days off and no jumping around. A one-way trip requires no backtracking, so I always looked forward to new territory ahead, but I couldn't sync my itinerary with local seasons in scattered parts of the globe, so I'd miss some bird-migration hotspots and hit other places during the not-ideal monsoons.

I set some ground rules. Every bird that I would count, for the whole year, would have to be seen by at least one other person. That would keep me from getting lonely, and, as a side benefit, would provide backup witnesses for each sighting. Also, I decided, my companions should all be locals, living in the same country where we went birding together. It would have been easy to hire professional guides from international tour companies to show me around, but that didn't exactly fit my style; I didn't have the budget, for one thing, and I'd always rather go out with friends than as a client. Connecting with locals became a key part of my strategy — this would be the couch-surfing version of birding trips.

A decade ago, such a concept would have been difficult to pull off, but technology has shrunk the world so that it's now easier to call someone up in another country than to get the attention of your roommate. The Internet has revolutionized birding: what was once a leisure pursuit for the First World has suddenly become a truly international pastime. Now anyone with an interest can find all kinds of helpful information online — and, even more important, get in touch with sympathetic souls through email lists, discussion groups, and forums.

Finding all of these local birders and arranging plans with each of them was a tricky logistical challenge. After settling my basic itinerary, I started looking for the best birders in each place who might be willing to host me for a few days. First I asked friends I already knew; then I asked them for their contacts, and so on. Some people were busy, but almost everyone replied with enthusiasm when I explained the project. To find Freddy, for instance, I first contacted a birder named Ignacio "Kini" Roesler, on the faculty of the University of Buenos Aires, who said he'd be busy with a Hooded Grebe research project in January, but he passed me on to a friend named

Nacho Areta. When I emailed Nacho, he replied that he'd be on a Mississippi Kite survey, but he gave me Freddy's email address — and so the match was made, with the friend of a friend of a friend.

In some places I used a website, BirdingPal, where people list themselves as willing hosts for birders traveling through their area. These aren't professional guides, but they offer hospitality and good company. It's fun to show off your local patch to someone who has never seen it, and favors get returned when the roles are reversed.

I also relied heavily for my planning on eBird, an online database of sightings started by the Cornell Lab of Ornithology and the National Audubon Society in 2002. With nearly half a billion observations logged by hundreds of thousands of birders around the world, the website has become an incredible resource on bird distribution and records, used by scientists to track bird migration and populations. eBird was a godsend for logistical planning: it helped me identify places where I was likely to find certain species, with up-to-the-minute reports, and showed which birders had been most active in areas I wanted to visit. Whenever the word-of-mouth method hit a dead end, I checked out eBird for new leads.

Crashing on couches seems like a casual approach, but setting up all of these visits took five solid months of intense planning. By the time I left home, I knew where I would be, and who I would be with, on nearly every day of 2015. The roster of birders had hundreds of names and kept growing as plans changed and the year progressed.

Nothing can replace local knowledge — of restaurants, shortcuts, customs, languages, secret spots, and the innumerable other things that only residents can tap into. By going with locals, I could instantly become an insider instead of a tourist; and by staying in people's homes instead of resorts and lodges, I could experience a big slice of real life on Earth without busting my bank account. Local knowledge would certainly pay off with birds that might otherwise be missed. But until the year began, I had no way of answering the question: Would it work?

Many of the people I contacted had no experience with guiding visitors; they came from all walks of life, spoke different languages, and ranged in age from their teens to their seventies. Each seemed to have a slightly different vision of what I was trying to do. Some of them wrote back immediately, while others took months to respond. In some cases, the only correspondence I'd had before landing in an unfamiliar country was through a Facebook message or WhatsApp chat. When I found myself blindly wiring money to personal bank accounts in sub-Saharan Africa and Southeast Asia, to cover expenses for upcoming trips to national parks with birders I'd never talked to on the phone and who replied to my emails in barely intelligible English, or in other languages entirely, I had a momentary panic attack. Was this a good idea? There was only one thing to do — trust and go forward.

Might as well have jumped in the river with the Torrent Ducks, I thought, as I slogged up the mule trail. Rain slashed down in sheets. For a while, I held grimly to an umbrella, but it was no use. Drops ricocheted off the ground, a gust of wind whipped the umbrella inside out, and wet vegetation lined the trail like the scrubbers at a car wash. At this point, it was impossible to get any wetter. I could have filled a pint glass with rainwater by wringing out my underwear.

Of more immediate concern, though, was the electricity in the air. Freddy, Claudia, José, Fabri, and I had hiked into a thunderstorm, not under it but *inside* it, and the atmosphere was charged with popping and crackling sounds as we ascended a ridge. Lightning and thunder became indistinguishable; in a cloud break I saw a bolt strike the valley underneath us, then the view snapped shut and we were left inside a swirling, horizonless world of strobe lights, reverberating concussions, and disorienting motion.

The rain pounded us. I no longer tried to step on bare ground; the rutted trail became a six-inch-deep cascade, and I sloshed upstream, hoping that the garbage bag lining my pack was at least keeping some stuff dry. Every time I looked up, wind stung my eyes, so I walked with my head down, water streaming off the tip of my nose, trying not to think of the estimated 20,000 people who get hit by lightning each year. Around a corner I almost bumped into Freddy, who had stopped to wait. He turned around, spread out his arms, looked up at the sky with a wild gleam in his eye, and said, *"Me gusta esta Cerro Negro!"* — I like it this way!

I had to admire his enthusiasm.

We arrived at our campsite, completely bedraggled, just before dark. The thunderstorm finally blew into the next valley, leaving behind a clear sky and curling tendrils of mist at sunset. Our mule driver had dumped piles of gear on a ridgetop, and we located several waterlogged tarps and tents, staked them to a grassy area, and dug into dinner. To feed five people for four days in the mountains, Freddy had packed biscuits, saltines, corned beef, tinned sardines, apples, peanuts, and candy, all of which were damp from the rain. Right now, it looked like a feast. At least water wasn't an issue — we gulped straight from a nearby stream, on hands and knees, until Freddy figured out how to drink out of a plastic shopping bag. Somehow, none of us had thought to bring a water bottle.

Thank goodness Freddy had brought an extra sleeping bag for me. After a brief *buenas noches*, I turned in early, looking forward to my first good sleep in several days. Inside my tent, I opened my backpack, untwisted the garbage bag inside, and discovered with delight that its contents were still fluffy and dry. I peeled off wet layers, put on dry ones, and promptly passed out. Weird, unidentifiable birds occupied my dreams all night long.

In the morning, groggy and slightly confused as to my where-abouts, I poked my head out of the tent flap to see an enormous Andean Condor glide by at eye level, swiveling its head as it passed. Ah, yes — Argentina. Fresh snow frosted the peaks around camp. The tent smelled like rain, the grass smelled like rain, the trees smelled like rain, the sopping clothes on our clothesline smelled like rain, and the view was magnificent. Layer upon layer of green ridges, cloaked in cloud forest, folded away in every direction. I checked my watch, but the battery had stopped; my cell phone was also dead, so there was no telling the time except by the sun, which emerged in one of the most brilliant dawn displays I'd ever seen.

The others also were stirring. Claudia strolled around camp, using her botanist's knowledge to forage for wild peaches, and sud-denly exclaimed, "Oh!"

"*Que pasó?*" called José, from inside his tent.

"*Una culebra,*" said Claudia, as she leaned over to inspect some-thing in the grass.

I wriggled into soaking wet pants, folded up the dry pair to sleep in, pulled on freezing wet socks and shoes, and padded over to check it out. A foot-long snake, marked by a repeating X pattern along its back, was curled up in a loose pretzel.

"*Bothrops,*" said Claudia, referring to the genus of pit vipers — highly venomous residents of Latin America — and motioned for me not to touch it. It was an attractive little snake with a boxy, trian-gular head, less than thirty feet from where I had just been resting, and it could bring down a horse. We left it well alone.

A few minutes later, as I chewed on whole sardines for break-fast, crunching their vertebrae and licking up the oil, an Aplomado Falcon kept an eye on us from its nearby perch. Freddy, munch-ing on a chocolate bar and stroking his pointy beard, explained our plan: the next two days would be spent hiking around the Pastizal grasslands, up to about 11,500 feet elevation, searching for seldom-seen birds with alluring names like Tucumán Mountain-Finch, Maquis Canastero, and Zimmer's Tapaculo, before we returned to be picked up at the trailhead the following afternoon. With luck, the rain-swollen river would subside and we could wade back across without having to swim the rapids.

Taking in the scene, I reflected on the benefits of going local. Organized tours never visited this place; when I later asked some professional guides about it, they'd never heard of Cerro Negro. It was too hard to reach, too difficult as a tourist destination. But the birds were here, and that's exactly why I had contacted Freddy — he knew the back corners of the Jujuy province in a way that no visitor ever could.

My system was working! I couldn't quite believe it. Two weeks into the year, nobody had stood me up yet; in fact, I was beginning to realize that birders were excited enough about this project to make elaborate plans and invite others along. This is what birding is all about — people with a shared passion, sometimes from entirely different continents and maybe not even speaking the same language, meeting as strangers, joining in a common goal, and becoming the best of friends. When I first emailed Freddy, I couldn't have predicted that we'd be standing on this mountain, the five of us, with three wet mules and a killer view.

He flashed a huge grin. The day was young, and we had birds to find.

"Okay, *vámanos!*" — let's go!

4

Over the Years

AS A KID, I wouldn't have been caught dead with a "history" book, but from the time I could barely read, at about the age of three, when I received a lovely picture book called *A Year of Birds*, I couldn't get enough stories about nature and adventure. Birding has a particularly wacky and wonderful lore, in books such as *The Big Year; The Big Twitch; The Biggest Twitch; Kingbird Highway; Lost Among the Birds; Birding on Borrowed Time; Call Collect, Ask for Birdman; The Ardent Birder; Extreme Birder; The Feather Quest; Wild America; Return to Wild America; To See Every Bird on Earth* — well, you get the idea.

I learned from reading bird books that nothing happens outside of historical context. In birding as in everything, personalities and events unfold over time, one thing leads to another, and pretty soon you wake up to discover that you are part of the stream.

Historically speaking, obsession with birds has often overlapped with a healthy sense of wanderlust. Seat-of-the-pants exploits feature prominently in the resumés of most early ornithologists, including

John James Audubon, who was inspired to track down the birds of North America with little more than a shotgun and a set of paints after being jailed for unpaid debts from a failed business venture in the early 1800s. For the next several years, Audubon traveled across the continent, living rough, studying (and shooting) every bird he could find, and created beautiful, meticulous illustrations of each species. The resulting folio of portraits, *Birds of America*, eventually earned him the respect he craved, but it was Audubon's swashbuckling tales from the frontier that made him truly famous — a real American hero.

Audubon wasn't the first by any means. The Scottish-American artist Alexander Wilson, sometimes called the "father of American ornithology," released nine volumes of bird paintings, literally drawing from his own intrepid travels, before Audubon had even stepped into the wilderness. And a full eighty years before that, the luminary British naturalist Mark Catesby included 220 plates of birds and other species in his *Natural History of Carolina, Florida, and the Bahama Islands*, the first published record of North America's flora and fauna. Just imagine Catesby's impressions when he landed on Virginia soil at the age of twenty-nine, in the spring of 1712, to spend the next seven years traipsing through the colonies. His illustrations included many species never before encountered by European naturalists.

But it wasn't until the mid-1900s that watching birds became an obsession unto itself, more like a sport than an art or science, and one man did more to popularize this new activity than anyone else.

His name was Roger Tory Peterson.

This is where modern birding really begins. The son of two immigrants in western New York, Peterson studied at the Art Students League and National Academy of Design in New York City. There, in the mid-1920s, he attended meetings of the Linnaean

Society, still active today, where amateur biologists gathered to talk about birds. He soon fell in with a group of teenage bird nerds who started their own group, the Bronx County Bird Club.

At the time, the best bird-identification guides were produced by Chester Reed, who supplied the nascent movement in nature study with illustrated pocket-sized guidebooks. The first, published in 1905, *Bird Guide: Land Birds East of the Rockies*, described nearly 220 species, with one color drawing on each page. Now bird enthusiasts could carry into the field a portable reference with color pictures of birds. Reed is largely forgotten today, but his importance cannot be overstated — he essentially created the first modern field guide, which Roger Tory Peterson, along with the rest of the Linnaean Society and Bronx County Bird Club members, used while scouting for birds around New York.

After graduating from art school in 1931, Peterson pursued his interest in identifying birds in the field — with binoculars instead of the shotgun used by earlier ornithologists such as Audubon. In the meantime, partly inspired by Reed's guides, he worked steadily on his own project. In 1934, a twenty-six-year-old Peterson published the book that would change birding forever.

A Field Guide to the Birds was something entirely new — so different from any previous book that several publishers rejected the idea, and Houghton Mifflin, the company that took the chance, committed to printing only 2,000 copies. The guide included Peterson's illustrations of all eastern North American birds, arranged with similar species side by side on plates, in various plumages, with arrows pointing out each distinctive feature. Unlike Audubon's *Birds of America*, which comprised four volumes, each weighing sixty pounds, Peterson's guide could be carried into the field; unlike Reed's little bird guides, Peterson's book was complete and showed multiple birds on each page.

When *A Field Guide* exhausted its first printing in one week, Peterson knew he had a hit, but it would take years for the full impact to sink in. He would live to edit, decades later, the book's fifth edition, by which time seven million copies had been sold. Peterson-branded nature guides, covering everything from birds to mushrooms, are the world's most successful series of field guides, all because of that first bird book in 1934.

In many ways, Peterson changed the way we look at the natural world. His field mark system offers encouragement, suggesting that any thorny problem can be solved by observing it closely enough. Not only did *A Field Guide* instruct its readers, but it also reflected a revolutionary shift in perspective. By simplifying each bird into its distinctive characteristics, Peterson made it possible for anyone, not just experts, to identify complicated targets — and thus brought birdwatching to the masses.

These books made Peterson famous. But one thing was still missing in his life: the rugged adventure that had become a tradition among earlier ornithologists. Peterson traveled often, but his work kept him so busy that he could never leave it all behind. At last, he hatched a plan with British seabird expert and friend James Fisher to take an extended trip across North America in 1953. The two devised a 30,000-mile route from Newfoundland to the tip of Florida, around the Gulf Coast to southern Texas and into Mexico, through Arizona and up the Pacific Coast to Washington, ending with a flight to the outer Pribilof Islands in Alaska. They set off in April and finished in July, exactly one hundred days later. Afterward, Peterson's commentary and Fisher's journal entries became a book, *Wild America*, a classic of environmental literature full of fascinating observations on everything from birds to alligators, fur seals, and 1950s America.

Wild America rode the swell of patriotic environmentalism that swept the United States in the 1950s, with birds at the heart of the story. The two naturalists introduced their readers to places that many had never heard of, inspiring more interest in the outdoors.

And near the end of the book, in small text at the bottom of a page, an intriguing footnote appeared.

"Incidental information: My year's list at the end of 1953 was 572 species (not counting an additional 65 Mexican birds)," wrote Peterson.

"Mine was 536, plus the 65 Mexican species, plus 117 others seen in Europe, a total of 718," added Fisher.

In fine print, a gauntlet had been thrown.

While Peterson and Fisher were crossing North America, another Mr. Fisher — this one named Dean, from Michigan — was headed for a U.S. Navy cruiser assigned to the Pacific Ocean. Dean Fisher was a bird enthusiast who tracked his sightings while sailing abroad. He'd seen about nine hundred bird species when he left the Navy in 1958, and he wasn't quite ready to settle down.

So he set off in 1959 with a friend on quite an adventure: they drove from California through Mexico, skirted Panama by freighter, and continued all the way to the southern tip of South America; then shipped their vehicle to South Africa, drove across the Sahara, sailed to Spain, and drove clear across Europe to reach India; then hitchhiked around the rest of southeast Asia for a while, sailed south, and finished with a long transect across northern Australia. It took three years.

Along the way, Fisher scouted for birds at every opportunity — local parks, swamps, forests, deserts. Many species he couldn't identify, because most countries had no published field guides at that time, but he kept detailed notes. It took a while — sometimes years — to identify what he had seen, but in the end he reckoned he'd passed 4,000 birds, more than 3,000 of them on this one round-the-world trip. In the year 1959 alone, he recorded 1,665 species, an unprecedented feat. Without really meaning to, he became the world's top bird lister.

Others were beginning to explore more far-flung places around the same time. Travel and tourism surged after World War II, thanks to new technology and an increasingly mobile population, and birders started to realize how many alluring species could be found beyond their own borders. Passenger jets began plying the skies in the late 1950s, cutting an overseas trip from five days to a few hours, and it wasn't long before intrepid ornithologists booked regular trips abroad.

One of them was young Peter Alden. During his studies at the University of Arizona in the mid-1960s, Alden spent five weeks each semester leading field trips across the border to Mexico with an emphasis on birds and local culture. After graduating, he went full-time and negotiated with the Massachusetts Audubon Society to lead a series of trips to even more exotic destinations. In 1968, he observed more than 2,000 species — a new single-year world record, surpassing Dean Fisher's 1959 tally — and helped pioneer international birding tourism, which would eventually become an industry of its own.

Perhaps the biggest advocate of birding abroad in those early days was an energetic Brit named Stuart Keith, who got hooked on birds while studying the classics at Oxford. Inspired by *Wild America*, Keith moved from England to California after graduating in 1955, then took careful aim at Roger Tory Peterson's North American single-year tally referenced in that fateful footnote. In 1956, the year he turned twenty-five, Keith drove across the United States and Canada with his brother, following a route similar to that of Peterson and Fisher but taking more time, and saw 594 species of birds — a new American Big Year record.

At the time, most ornithologists thought the world held about 8,600 bird species, and Keith began to wonder how many one person could see in a lifetime. As he took birding trips and got to know other keen birders, such as Roger Tory Peterson and Peter Alden, he realized that they were wondering the same thing.

Recognizing a critical mass when he saw it, Keith cofounded the American Birding Association in 1968 and became its first president, working with a friend, Jim Tucker, to produce a magazine they called *Birding*. Despite its focus on North America, the club's members — which numbered 115 after the first year, more than 500 a few months later, and about 13,000 today — did not confine themselves to the United States. In the early days, the association was all about listing, anywhere and everywhere. Initially it was an exclusive club: to join, prospective members had to have identified at least 500 species in North America or 70 percent of the birds in their home state, and people mailed in their list totals to determine a pecking order.

By the early 1970s, Keith had become the world's biggest lister, surpassing Dean Fisher's achievements in the late 1950s, and set his sights on a landmark goal. Several well-traveled birders, including Roger Tory Peterson, had decided to try to see half the birds in the world — about 4,300 species, according to prevailing wisdom — and Keith wanted to be the first to cross the threshold. He officially passed it in 1973, at age forty-one, having spent years slogging through some of the world's most rugged and remote corners. (Peterson would also reach half, but not until the mid-1980s.) Keith became a minor birding celebrity, hailed as a "superstar" by *People* magazine.

In a tantalizing article called "Birding Planet Earth: A World Overview," published in *Birding* magazine, Keith reflected on his experiences. "Getting to 'half' was the most exciting moment of my birding career," he wrote. "For the tireless and dedicated world

birder who simply cannot rest until he has seen a kiwi and a casso-
wary, and for those other addicts for whom visions of jabirus dance
in their heads, we may establish 4,300 species as a possible lifetime
goal. It took me 26 years."

He also made some predictions for his own future.

"I think I can just make it to 6,000, though I may be in a wheel-
chair when I do it," Keith calculated.

As it turned out, he exceeded that goal. He continued to travel
for the next thirty years before succumbing to a stroke in early
2003 on the Micronesian island of Chuuk, during a birding trip.
The day before, he had seen a Caroline Islands Ground-Dove, life
bird number 6,600.

In his article, Keith had considered the possibility of a one-
year global birding adventure.

"This is a big subject and worth an article in itself," Keith wrote,
"so rather than treat it here I would like to invite readers to send in
some theoretical models of global routes detailed month by month.
The appropriate person to write on the subject would be the reign-
ing world annual list champion, Peter Alden, who has several times
gone over 2,000. How about it, Peter? Could you do 3,000?"

To me, this paragraph is radical. It is the first printed reference
I can find to a world Big Year — not just an incidental one, but a
whole calendar year specifically designed to maximize species on a
planetary scale. Keith inspired others but never went for a global
Big Year himself, explaining that he preferred "to go to one area
and work it thoroughly."

Birdwatchers began to ask: How many birds in the world could
you really see in a year, no holds barred?

✦—✦—✦

The birders who survived the early 1970s tend to look back on those
years with wistfulness, using words like "innocence" and "golden

- -

age." A lot of things came together: Birders realized they were part of a larger community and began to share information with one another on a broad scale. New regional clubs made it easier to connect, and the pursuit was young enough that anyone could contribute to ornithological knowledge.

"Birding changed from a mild local pastime to a continent-wide craze," American birder Kenn Kaufman would write years later, reflecting on that era. "It is only now, looking back from a distance of two decades, that we can see how far-reaching and thorough the changes were . . . Birding for the twenty-first century was born in the brief period from 1970 to 1975."

Kaufman was a long-haired nineteen-year-old high school dropout when, in 1973, he spent an action-packed year hitchhiking long distances around the United States to chase birds — partly inspired by Peterson's *Wild America*. North American Big Years suddenly became trendy: a young prodigy named Ted Parker surpassed Stuart Keith's old record by seeing 626 species in 1971; then both Kaufman and American educator Floyd Murdoch set out to beat Parker's total two years later. It was the first time two people tried to set a birdwatching record in the same year, introducing a new element: competition.

Kingbird Highway, Kaufman's memoir published in 1997, is a manifesto of unfiltered passion. Kaufman often slept under bridges and practiced draconian frugality to survive on less than a dollar a day; one memorable passage describes Little Friskies cat food as a cheap and nutrient-filled dinner alternative. Though he set out to look for birds, Kaufman found himself swept up in the growing flock of avian admirers and, by the end of 1973, cemented a place for himself within this larger community. That he set a fresh American record of 666 species, only to be edged out by Murdoch's 669 that year, was of such diminished importance to him that he included the totals only as an afterthought, in an appendix.

Kingbird Highway had a profound effect on me when I first read it as a twelve-year-old. I was hungry for exotic stories. Here was a guy who refused to follow the typical path, a rebel, choosing instead to chase birds wherever they might lead. Such is the power of words that *Wild America* inspired a teen-aged Kaufman to start a birding revolution, and Kaufman's *Kingbird Highway* solidified my own dreams.

By the 1980s, North American Big Years were well established among hardcore birders, and it became clear that the domestic record was up for grabs. A Mississippi businessman, James Vardaman, sensing an opportunity to raise publicity for his forestry firm, hired a team of bird experts to guide him around North America for a year and ended with 699 species — showing what a "lousy birder but a great promoter," as Vardaman described himself, might do with enough money, time, and expert guidance. During his quest, Vardaman flew 137,145 miles, sometimes catching a plane just to chase one stray bird reported on the opposite side of the continent, and drove another 20,305 miles. His strategy set the tone for later efforts, when a few dedicated souls would push well past 700 species and even, in the new millennium, 750 in a year, but this willy-nilly style — ticking one rare, vagrant bird at a time after listing all the common ones, burning massive amounts of fuel for vastly diminishing returns on one continent — has completely diverged from the pastime of wandering through a forest just to see what's there.

Perhaps Vardaman was thinking of this disconnect when, in the final paragraph of his book, *Call Collect, Ask for Birdman*, he abruptly shifted his gaze to all of planet Earth.

"I will definitely start planning a World Big Year," he wrote. "But because of the distances and complexities involved, planning a World Big Year will take some years, and executing the plan will take 365 days and probably cost $700,000 even at present prices. Therefore, I couldn't make the try before 1985, and I'll be glad to turn the plan over to someone else if I can't carry it out. Is 5,000 possible?"

Heaven only knows what Vardaman had in mind with that budget estimate (his $700,000 in 1980 would inflate to more than $2 million by the time I embarked on my worldwide adventure), but at least he was thinking big. He did travel enough to net 2,800 species and a new official worldwide record in 1984, even if he never got around to a coordinated international assault.

The only person who achieved a higher one-year total in that generation was James Clements, a maverick ornithologist who literally wrote the book on birds of the world. For his doctoral thesis at California Western University, Clements authored the global checklist still used by most American birders (including me), which standardizes names for every bird species on Earth. He then operated a printing business, which allowed him to travel a lot, and in 1989 set out to see as many birds as he could, using the Big Year concept to raise funds for the Los Angeles Museum of Natural History. By the end of the year, Clements had covered more than 265,000 miles and recorded 3,662 bird species, at one point getting himself arrested in West Africa for stalking a hornbill "without permission." He raised $50,000 for the museum. Afterward, he continued to study birds abroad until he died in 2005, leaving the Cornell Lab of Ornithology the task of maintaining his world checklist.

Today, James Clements is remembered as one of birding's most passionate proponents and explorers, with a species of Peruvian gnatcatcher named in his honor, and few people even know about his 1989 Big Year. That record stood quietly for almost twenty years. By the time anyone could take a serious crack at it, birding itself was undergoing a global revolution.

+ - + - +

When Clements took his round-the-world jaunt, I was a three-year-old. I am part of the digital generation, a so-called millennial — the world's first cohort to grow up online, coming of age around the year 2000. Culturally speaking, we millennials are significantly different from the baby boomers or even Generation X: we're more progressive, less religious, more educated, less family-oriented, more urban, less political, more narcissistic, less environmentally minded, and, above all, more technologically dependent. For better or worse, my generation lives on computers and smartphones; we are children of the Internet.

So how do you explain the surging allure of birdwatching in recent years? If nobody cared about the environment anymore, you'd expect outdoor activities to slack off — but, strangely, they've never been more popular. A 2014 *Esquire* magazine headline said it best: "Uh-Oh. Birdwatching Is About to Become Cool." When, in short order, Owen Wilson plays a real-life birder in a Hollywood movie about birding, Jonathan Franzen writes an angsty feature about birds for *The New Yorker*, and rock star Geddy Lee is quoted saying "I'm a birder, believe it or not," you know something's up.

It's tempting to suggest that birdwatching is a backlash against technology, that getting back to nature responds to a deep, intangible human need, and I'd like to think that people are willingly seeking outdoor therapy to balance their new digital lifestyles. But it's probably the other way around — all this technology and connectedness has changed the way people enjoy birds and nature, engaging us in new and exciting ways. Ironically, going online is inspiring us to go outside.

For birders, the Information Age revolutionized the way we communicate with each other — through dedicated email lists, discussion groups, and websites like BirdingPal, eBird, and BirdForum. Instead of a niche activity for wealthy retirees, birdwatching has been transformed into a truly international popular pursuit.

Outside the United States and Europe, places like Brazil, India, and the Philippines are adding their own cultural twists to the appreciation of birds. In China, for instance, birding is now seen as an aspirational activity — a sign of elite class, because you must have enough money for binoculars and spotting scopes, as well as leisure time to do it. Ten years ago there were virtually no birders in the entire country, but bird groups have suddenly sprung up on most Chinese university campuses and in most major cities.

At the same time, technology has made it easier to learn about birds. Digital cameras make identification a breeze, while binoculars have become so good that manufacturers worry customers will never replace them. Field guides are available nearly everywhere, and they're increasingly available as smartphone apps. The Cornell Lab of Ornithology has an app, Merlin, that identifies the bird species in your photograph with about 80 percent accuracy. Another program does the same for bird songs: hold up your phone and it names the unseen singer, like Shazam for bird calls.

We are now at the point where it is about as easy to travel the world as it was to explore the United States in the 1970s, during the previous revolution in birdwatching.

In 2008, two British birders, Ruth Miller and Alan Davies, decided to take on Clements's record from 1989. A lot had happened in the intervening nineteen years, and they thought it was time for someone to revive the world Big Year idea. Miller and Davies took their adventure seriously, planning discrete trips to rack up as many species as they could, and they sold their house to pay for it. By the end of the year, the two had seen 4,341 species of birds together in more than twenty countries, smashing Clements's old tally and showing what was possible in this new, networked age.

I followed their progress closely and scoured their book, *The Biggest Twitch*, for insights on how to improve their global strategy. Miller and Davies flew home between each destination, skipped around, missed some key areas, and spent a whopping three months in Europe, which has the fewest birds of any of the six major continents. I wondered if someone would put together an even bigger Big Year, and how they might approach it.

That spring, I graduated from college and had my sights set on remote research stints with various bird projects. As the global economy crashed, I rode it out in a subfreezing tent in Antarctica, strapping GPS tags to penguins and tracking their movements as part of a long-term study. If you had told me then that I would be the one to assault the all-time world Big Year record a few years later, I would have laughed. But now, looking back, I can see that the seeds of a plan were already sprouting in the back of my mind.

5

The Harpy

BY LATE JANUARY, the days had begun to speed up and blur into each other. After leaving Freddy and *amigos* in Jujuy, my plan was to blitz through northeast Argentina, then spend the next three weeks racing through the birdiest parts of Brazil with a relay of excellent local contacts.

In Argentina I joined up with a gung-ho birder named Guy Cox to rattle around the Misiones province in his newly acquired 1974 Chevy camper van. Our meeting was slightly delayed on account of a broken drive shaft that had to be fixed, which gave me a morning to explore the spectacular Iguazu Falls, a two-mile-wide cataract best described as "Niagara on Viagra," as well as Iguazu's specialty bird species — a flock of Great Dusky Swifts that nest behind the falls. Then Guy and I trundled down red dirt roads to the nearby San Sebastian de la Selva forest reserve, a little-known gem where we ditched the hordes of tourists and found ourselves surrounded instead by tropical birds: antshrikes, antvireos, antwrens, antthrushes, antpipits, antpittas, and ant-tanagers.

At last, I'd reached the tropics, complete with unrelenting heat and humidity, cloying mud, brightly colored macaws, all manner of vines and fronds, titi monkeys . . . and ants. The northeast corner of Argentina forms the western boundary of a wet, muggy jungle called the Atlantic Rainforest, which stretches in a narrow belt 2,500 miles along the coast to eastern Brazil. The forest is isolated by dry savannas to the north, so it's a hotspot for endemic plants and animals: more than 150 species of Atlantic Rainforest birds are found nowhere else. Unfortunately, it is also one of the world's most degraded environments, and virtually all of the Brazilian section of the forest has been chopped down. A system of reserves protects the Argentinian side, which means that while historically only 4 percent of this forest was outside of Brazil, today about 50 percent of what's left of it is in Argentina.

Guy and I prowled the jungle, looking and listening for specialty birds. With Guy's local knowledge and incredible ear, we found many, including a gleaming blue-black-green-red Surucua Trogon on January 22 that marked my first big milestone — the 500th bird of the year. Only 4,500 to go.

I said *adiós* to Guy, then crossed the Brazilian border by taxi and flew onward to São Paulo. Brazil was a key strategic stop, but as a United States citizen, it was not easy for me to get in because of an ongoing visa spat. In most countries I got tourist visas, for a fee, online or upon arrival. But to enter Brazil, U.S. citizens must procure a travel visa ahead of time at a Brazilian consulate, which entails showing up at an appointed time with a completed application form, extra photo, valid passport, copy of a round-trip ticket, and U.S. Postal Service money order for the full price (no cash or check). This is all payback for the United States government's tightening its visa requirements for Brazil and other nations in 2001.

Of the many visas I had to get, the one for Brazil was by far the most complicated and expensive. In the end, I had to buy a second passport and hire the specialists at VisaHQ to sort out the visa morass. I would shell out more than $2,000 on visas during the year.

In Brazil I hooked up for a couple days of birding with Guto Carvalho, a birder and film producer who sold his production house several years ago to focus on special projects and conservation. Guto used to commute to Hollywood and New York to work on special effects for commercials and films. Now he travels around South America to give talks about birds, runs the annual Brazil Bird Fair, organizes regional bird fairs in other states, and operates a small editorial house that publishes nature and photography books. He had recently wrapped an animated TV series about sustainability and would be off in a couple of weeks to northern Brazil to work on a book about Amazonian bird life. Partly because of a dedicated core of birders and conservationists like Guto, a grassroots birding culture is rapidly growing in Brazil.

"Ten years ago there were almost no birders in Brazil," he told me as we left behind the lights of São Paulo near midnight, "but now we have lots of them around the country."

Guto and I visited Intervales State Park, one of the last significant remaining patches of Atlantic Rainforest. There, with the help of park guide Luis Avelino — who called out bird names in Latin — we saw more than 120 species in one exceptional day. At dinner that evening, it struck me that birding had brought together a very unlikely trio: a Brazilian film producer (Guto), a rural forest guide (Luis), and a twenty-eight-year-old bird man from Oregon (me). None of us would have had any other reason to know each other, and Luis spoke only Portuguese, yet we connected instantly and effortlessly with our shared interest in birds.

Guto passed me on to René Santos, a thirty-four-year-old birder also from São Paulo, who had a Spix's Macaw tattooed on his left shoulder, and the phrase "Extinction Is Forever" written in Portuguese on the spare tire of his seventeen-year-old Jeep. Tall and athletic, a disciple of surfing and the Brazilian martial art form of capoeira, René took me up the coast to the island of Ilhabela — literally, "beautiful island" — where we stayed at a friend's house and walked for hours through the hot, sticky lowland forest, searching for a few final regional endemics. Seeing a near-threatened Spot-breasted Antvireo was almost as sweet as the celebratory açaí ice cream, with sliced bananas and honey on top.

René dropped me at the São Paulo airport with good wishes, and I winged north, looking forward to a change of scenery. In ten full days of birding with Guy, Guto, and René across various sections of the Atlantic Rainforest, I had slept in ten different places. My few clothes desperately needed a wash, sweated out from a week and a half of slogging through the moist and mucky jungle, but I had trouble mustering the energy even to rinse them in the sink. All these quick transitions from one spot to the next — driving late, arriving in the middle of the night, getting up in the dark to start birding at dawn — were wearing me out, and sleep took priority over laundry, which wouldn't have dried anyway.

I scheduled most of my travel segments during afternoons and evenings to preserve the precious morning hours for birding, but I had no idea whether this itinerary would be sustainable. Besides the lack of sleep, I had no downtime, no alone time, and no rest. Whenever I moved to a new place, a new local birder was ready to go, and the effect was like constantly swapping in fresh horses for the Pony Express. I had another eleven months to go. Could I keep this up? Should I pace myself more? The great benefit of going nonstop is that new sights, people, and birds are always ahead, and an exhilarating jolt comes with each transition. Despite experiencing some torpor in the tropics, I was glad I had planned one continuous journey because I enjoyed the rush and didn't really want it to end. At this point, I was adjusting to the routine, relying more and more on the kinetic energy of new ground to keep me going. Increasingly, rest seemed to me a bad idea — it would break the flow, stop the roller coaster. Better to just keep riding.

After almost a month on the run, things were going fantastically well. None of the things I most feared had happened. I had not been sick. There had been no serious logistical nightmares. None of the local birders had let me down. And I was racking up birds faster than I'd dared to hope. Despite the slow start in Antarctica, by January 29 I had recorded 617 species, well above the daily average needed to reach 5,000 by the end of the year. It was early days yet, but I could feel the Big Year momentum building. The sun seemed to be shining a new light on the world, and nothing could overshadow my happiness. Maybe it couldn't last, but so far, so good.

Then, upon landing in the city of Cuiabá in central Brazil, I received some unexpected and exciting news.

✦ - ✦ - ✦

Deep in central Brazil, in the sprawling state of Mato Grosso near the Bolivian border, lies an obscure range of low mountains called Serra das Araras. The landscape here is squeezed between powerful forces. To the north, the Amazon — the world's largest rainforest — runs all the way to Guyana and eastern Ecuador. To the south and east is the Cerrado, an interior plateau about the size of Greenland, with tropical savannas to rival the wide-open vistas of east Africa. And to the west, the famous Pantanal floods a seasonal wetland the size of Spain. The headwaters of the Paraguay River trickle down from the Serra das Araras; follow the flow and you'll drift 1,700 miles across the Pantanal and into Argentina, merge with the Paraná River, and continue another lazy eight hundred miles to the Atlantic Ocean somewhere north of Buenos Aires.

West-central Brazil is a long way from anywhere, and amid this trifecta — Amazon, Cerrado, and Pantanal — the Serra das Araras doesn't get much attention from foreigners. The escarpment isn't dramatically scenic or touristy, though you can stay at a small Brazilian inn called a *pousada* with a spa and cozy rooms next to grazing cattle and a limestone mine. It's sizzlingly hot and sticky, and the access highway from Cuiabá, the nearest big city, has so much heavy truck traffic that the pavement resembles hardened Conestoga wagon ruts.

As darkness fell, I bumped down this road with Giuliano Bernardon, a young bird guide, and his sister Bianca, a biologist visiting from the north Brazilian province of Amazonas. They had picked me up after I touched down in Cuiabá on a late afternoon flight. Once we crossed the city limits, the highway ran straight as a parrot can fly. The landscape was flat, flat, flat, and it was crowded with trucks, trucks, trucks. Roadside tire shops popped up every couple of miles, evidently doing brisk business owing to the many potholes and ruts. After sunset we were left in a jarring, terrifying tunnel of oncoming headlights and black holes, and I was relieved when Giuliano decided to stop in the tiny town of Jangada for dinner and a few hours of sleep. We had originally planned to head straight for the Pantanal, but when Giuliano met me at the airport he had some good news.

"There is an active Harpy Eagle nest at Serra das Araras!" he said, before we'd even made it across the parking lot. "It isn't exactly on the way — more of a side trip — but we can be there at dawn tomorrow."

Giuliano wore a broad smile, dark beard, and mustache, and was outfitted in loose layers of khaki and a wide-brimmed hat. He explained that some visiting birders had confirmed a female sitting on the nest just a few days before, so we had a good chance of stak-

ing out the elusive eagle. It might be only one species for my Big
Year total, but it was worth spending an extra morning for a chance
to see the most powerful raptor in the Western Hemisphere.

Three feet tall, with a seven-foot wingspan and weighing up
to twenty pounds, the Harpy is a Sherman tank with fighter-jet
wings. Early South American explorers named this bird after the
Harpies of Greek mythology — ravenous beasts with a bird's body
and a woman's face, sent by Zeus to snatch people off the face of the
Earth — and the comparison is apt. Harpy Eagles prey mainly on
monkeys and sloths, plucked unceremoniously from treetops, and
can take down red brocket deer and other large rainforest animals,
given the chance. To do so, they have evolved enormous talons,
longer than the claws of a grizzly bear, and powerful legs as thick
as a child's wrist. Females are nearly twice the size of males, as with
most of the world's eagle species.

These creatures are stunning to behold, with large crests and
bold black-and-white plumage, and have no trouble speeding
through a dense canopy at fifty miles per hour, exploding onto their
targets in a burst of speed and raw power. Monkeys have learned to
let go when they see a Harpy Eagle coming, preferring to drop like a
stone to the forest floor rather than confront such a fearsome predator at canopy level, but by then it's usually too late. Harpies are
masters of surprise and disguise, adapted to close combat in jungle
environments. They are the ultimate avian predator.

Harpies are also quite rare, as they need large tracts of intact
forest in which to live and breed. One pair generally requires several thousand acres of pristine rainforest, which is hard to come
by. Habitat loss has threatened the species throughout most of its
historic range, from southern Mexico to northern Argentina, and
Harpies are now found in appreciable numbers only in the wildest
parts of the Amazon basin, including northern Brazil.

Even in the most untouched, remote forests, Harpies are exasperatingly difficult to glimpse. They have evolved cryptic behaviors, skulking through the canopy rather than soaring overhead, in order not to spook potential prey — which means you either need to get extremely lucky to spot one or stake one out at a nest.

While we ate fried sandwiches at an open-air food cart in Jangada, surrounded by hungry truckers, Giuliano explained that the Harpy Eagle nest at Serra das Araras has been used for about twenty years, since the mid-1990s. Many birders have seen their first wild Harpy at this site. The eagles take two years to raise their chicks, and the nest is used irregularly — at most once every other year. A few other nests are scattered elsewhere in Brazil, but the birds aren't always present, and none of the others seemed to be active during my visit. So this would be my only real chance for a view of the near-mythical bird.

Giuliano and Bianca checked us into a small hotel and, with a brief *boa noite*, left me in my room with instructions to be ready at 4:45 a.m. for the eagle search. I dropped my backpack in a corner, sat on the bed, and switched on the TV. It had only a few stations, all in Portuguese, and I couldn't understand much. As I pulled out my laptop, propped up on a pillow, and typed some notes for the day, a Brazilian newscast droned in the background.

It felt strange to be touring the world and yet to be so detached from it. In the previous week, unknown to me, the president of Yemen had resigned, people were massacred in Nigeria, Swiss banks caused turmoil in the financial markets, the U. S. Senate approved the controversial Keystone XL pipeline, and the Ebola crisis escalated in West Africa. Before leaving home a month earlier I'd paid close attention to the global news, sensing that I'd soon be out there *inside* the headlines. But the reality was just the opposite: here in a tiny village in central Brazil, the news felt very far away indeed. Now that I was actually traveling the planet, each day deepening my connection with its great wealth of birds and birders, the media stories seemed to apply to some completely different universe — one in which I had no part. The time I spent searching for each bird was so intense — heightened by the knowledge that I would soon leave and move on — that it seemed to swallow up all the available space. Disoriented, I gradually fell into a restless sleep of uneasy dreams.

When my alarm went off several hours later, it took a minute to adjust to my surroundings. Then I remembered: Harpy day! I grabbed my backpack, stumbled out the door into the dark, and met Giuliano and Bianca. We threw our gear in the truck and drove toward the eagle stakeout, ready for action.

In light traffic at 4:45 a.m., we made efficient time, arriving at Serra das Araras just after dawn. The rutted pavement gave way to dirt, then disappeared entirely into a grassy cow pasture. Giuliano carefully picked out a parking spot amidst the cows and cowpats, and led the way on foot for the last few hundred yards.

Birds were everywhere among the clearings and forest patches as the sun rose. Lettered Aracaris, a type of small, colorful toucan, played hide-and-seek among the foliage, while Yellow-tufted Woodpeckers chased each other in playful circles around a snag. A dark Bat Falcon, no bigger than a flying beer bottle, streaked overhead. Thrush-like Wrens chattered noisily from the thickets, a Blue-headed Parrot admired the view from the top of a tall tree, and a Ferruginous Pygmy-Owl called from a distance. Almost every bird was new for my year list, this being my first morning in central Brazil, but they were all common species I expected to see again in the coming weeks. I had one target here and, as the moment arrived, I could barely contain my excitement.

A massive tree materialized in front of us. About two-thirds of the way up, in a three-way fork in the trunk, I beheld a nest the size of a Volkswagen bus — a platform of sticks big enough for me to lie down inside, had it not been inhabited by one of the world's most ferocious creatures. These eagles had built themselves a magnificent fortress in the sky. I raised my binoculars, focused on the spot, and saw, poking above the rim of the nest . . .

Nothing. No Harpies.

This was obviously the right spot, but where were the eagles?

"Hmmm," said Giuliano, after a minute of steady inspection. "Bianca, do you see anything?"

"Nope," she replied. "All I see is the nest."

The three of us stared upward. Birds twittered and sang all around us, but we were focused only on the one that wasn't home.

"They were here last week," said Giuliano, looking perplexed. "A group of birders stopped here and reported the female sitting on the nest, and even watched the male fly in with some food. So it has to be active. Let's try a different angle — maybe she's in there right now but is sitting too low so we can't see her."

We edged around the tree, maintaining an equal radius from its trunk, until we reached the opposite side. No eagles, though the nest itself, from this new angle, was still impressive enough. Imagine building a treehouse, piece by piece, without being able to use your arms! What a load of work.

"Hmmm," Giuliano repeated. "They must be around here somewhere. Let's wait awhile and see if one of the eagles turns up. Maybe they're out getting breakfast."

For one of these birds, popping out for breakfast would likely mean murdering a monkey — an indelicate thought, barbarous even. Did they ever wake up and reflect on this stuff?

We settled down on a fallen log to wait. Giuliano and Bianca sat next to each other in matching outfits: pastel green shirts, field pants, knee-high rubber boots, and sun hats. Giuliano, as a full-time bird guide, knew this site well and seemed completely at ease as he kept up a pleasant banter about birds, culture, and food. Bianca, meanwhile, had just traveled down from northern Brazil, where she worked as a bird researcher in the Amazon rainforest, and her eyes lit up every time a new species was spotted. Brother and sister picked off one sighting after another, and I scrambled to keep up.

"Scaled Pigeon!" said Giuliano, and aimed his spotting scope at a distant treetop to get a better view. Magnified thirty times, I could see the pigeon's red bill, brown body, and namesake pattern of intricate marks on the side of its neck like silhouetted snake skin.

"And an Epaulet Oriole," interrupted Bianca, pointing out an all-black bird with bright yellow shoulder patches.

A few minutes later we observed a Red-necked Woodpecker, one of the largest woodpeckers in the world, sidling up a dead tree like a feathered jackhammer, and later heard its echoing double-knock display. Then a Black-throated Saltator — distinguished by its orange bill and black face — made a cameo, and I pondered the benefits of birding in overlap zones. The woodpecker is a true Amazon bird while the saltator is confined mostly to the central Brazilian Cerrado. But here, where the two biomes meet, birds from both habitats could be seen side by side.

As the sun climbed into a fiercely blue sky, Bianca was telling me about her research in the Amazonas province, where she was about to begin a Ph.D. project studying Black Skimmers — strange, tern-like birds that drag their elongated lower bill through the water to snap up fish midflight — when suddenly she broke off and pointed to a distant line of trees. "Hey, what's that white speck?" she asked.

All three of us trained our binoculars on the spot, which appeared to be a large bird perched on a limb. It had the hulking shape of a raptor, with stooped shoulders and a fierce-looking gestalt, just far enough away that we couldn't quite discern the details. Giuliano lined up his spotting scope, took a look, and stepped back with a slow smile.

"It's . . . an . . . eagle . . ." he began.

My heart skipped. I leaned forward to peer through the eyepiece. Staring back at me was a big, mean-looking bird with a black back, all-white chest, white head, yellow eyes, black mask, and orange bill.

". . . but it's not a Harpy," Giuliano said. "That's a Black-and-white Hawk-Eagle, which is a big bonus for us! These are really rare and unpredictable — we don't have any nest sites or stakeouts for Black-and-white Hawk-Eagles, so it's lucky to come across one in the forest."

Were we lucky? I wasn't sure whether to be ecstatically happy or disappointed. The Harpy, which would have been almost twice as tall and ten times heavier, remained at large, but in any other circumstance this hawk-eagle would have made my day. It was a neat, crisp-looking bird, dressed in sharp lines and stark contrasts, and I spent a long time studying its features through the scope. The Black-and-white Hawk-Eagle preys on all kinds of animals, but its main diet is other, smaller birds, so it has to be quick and agile. Eventually, this one fanned its tail, flashing a neat barred pattern, and disappeared into the forest. It really was a rare sighting. I wouldn't see another for the rest of the year.

After my heart rate had returned to normal, I sat back down on the log to resume the Harpy Eagle vigil. An hour passed. Conversation died. The same smaller birds bounced around us — aracaris, woodpeckers, pigeons — and I watched them, getting to know them while keeping one eye peeled for a freakishly large raptor. I supposed the other birds were keeping an eye out, too, never knowing when an attack might come from above. For me, this was a fun way to spend a morning, but for the other creatures of the forest, eagle-watching was a never-ending fact of life.

Two hours passed, then three. Giuliano and Bianca looked a bit nervous, and I couldn't help checking my watch. How much time could we afford on one species, even if it was a Harpy? Strategically, spending more than an hour looking for a single bird was counterproductive. I chided myself for making these calculations;

surely anyone could see that a Harpy Eagle is worth more than the usual effort. But as we crept toward the four-hour mark, and my stomach started to worry about lunch, I wondered what else might be sacrificed if the guest of honor didn't appear soon.

As much as anything, our Harpy Eagle stakeout served to remind me that birding, like so many other pursuits — crossword puzzles, police work, space travel — is a game of patience punctuated by sharp moments of excitement. The thrill comes in unexpected doses. If birds were completely predictable, it would no longer be fun to look for them. Waiting is part of the addiction: the longer you wait and the more you hope, the bigger the payoff — even if that payoff never comes.

People like me get hooked on the birding habit in part because of the random payoffs, or what American psychologist B. F. Skinner described in the 1950s as a "variable ratio schedule." Skinner showed, in his now-famous operant-conditioning experiments, that mice can be taught to press a lever for treats, but that they become much more addicted to pressing the lever if they are sometimes rewarded with big treats, sometimes with small ones, and sometimes with nothing at all. Humans share this behavioral quirk; perversely, getting rewarded every time is not as fun as hitting the jackpot every once in a while. Casinos offer a classic example of random reinforcement: they have figured out how to exploit the way our brains are wired. Imagine a slot machine that, without fail, spit out ninety cents every time you put in a dollar. What's the fun in that? Switch it up, though, so that the machine occasionally pays more and sometimes gives you nothing, and, *voilà*, the game is irresistible.

Birding is exactly the same. For each moment of excitement, the brain gets a hit of dopamine — the neurotransmitter that controls pleasure — which reinforces all kinds of habit-forming behaviors. Research has shown that the more unexpected the reward, the more dopamine is released, which makes sense in the context of Skinner's variable schedules. But that's not quite the full story, because these chemicals can flood the system long before rewards actually occur; dopamine starts to kick in when we first *anticipate* a reward. This semi-stressful state keeps us curious and engaged. In other words, chemistry makes the search for birds as fun as the discovery.

All of which is a roundabout way of validating an otherwise irrational behavior like sitting for four hours in a remote Brazilian forest in a one-sided appointment with a wild bird. As lunchtime drew closer, I kept thinking, "The Harpy Eagle could appear at any moment if we just stay here a little longer!"

When the eagle came, it arrived silently, gliding directly over our heads on rigid wings. Giuliano, Bianca, and I had just decided to wait fifteen more minutes before packing it in, which felt a lot like admitting defeat.

"We need to move on toward the Pantanal," Giuliano said, in as soothing a tone as he could muster. "There are lots of other birds to find."

I could read the disappointment in his eyes, a reflection of the gutted feeling in my own chest. A Harpy might count the same as a sparrow for the Big Year, but to miss such a spectacular bird at such a promising location, after sitting for hours, didn't bear thinking about. I couldn't believe we'd blown half a day for zilch. Then, as if riding this emotional climax for its grand entrance, the mythical creature simply appeared, and any disappointment evaporated in a nanosecond.

My first thought was, "Whoa, that's a big bird!" The eagle swooped low toward the nest tree and flared into a stall, landing softly on a thick branch, facing away from us. Then it swiveled its head, fixed us with a hard stare, and turned its body around so that we could see the underside. From the front, I could admire the two powerful talons, which clutched something furry.

"It's got a snack," I said, while Giuliano aimed his spotting scope on the spot.

"Yeah," he replied. "I can't quite tell what it is. Here, take a look."

The Harpy Eagle was so big that it completely filled the scope view, so magnified that each feather was crisply delineated. I could see its black chest band, a spiky crest on top of its head, the hooked beak, and black and white bars on the wings and tail. The overall coloring was of charcoal, ash, and ink, and the bird's eyes were deep black without highlights. Size and plumage indicated an adult male, relatively small compared to a female — as if you could call it anything but enormous. There was nothing subtle in the expression of this Harpy.

Close inspection showed that the bird was holding some kind of animal with a long, striped tail hanging loosely underneath.

"What do you think of the prey?" I asked, swapping out with Giuliano and Bianca for extended looks through the scope.

We ruled out the local monkeys, which have plain-colored tails, before deciding that the only possible match was a coati, a raccoon-like animal widespread in the American tropics. This particular coati was past caring about its fate; it had already been partially consumed and seemed to be missing its head. Evidently the male Harpy Eagle had eaten half its lunch before transporting the leftovers, perhaps intending to share it with his mate. But where was his mate? Off hunting on her own somewhere? Hidden inside the nest? The male seemed uncertain, swiveling his head back and forth as if looking for her. He made no move to eat. He perched quietly, waiting for her to appear. How ironic, I thought. After we waited four hours for this eagle to show up, he was now waiting for someone else.

For such a large bird, he was oddly inconspicuous. If I hadn't seen him swoop overhead, it would have been easy to miss the shadowy shape sitting under the canopy, partially concealed by layers of foliage. The Harpy is a sneaky surprise-attack artist, and the half-eaten coati in his talons had probably not known its fate until the last instant.

After our allotted fifteen minutes stretched into an hour, the male eagle showed no signs of budging from its perch, and the female eagle showed no signs of appearing. I reluctantly let Giuliano fold up his scope.

"We have a long drive ahead," he said, "and a few other species to look for before dark."

Still, I hesitated. I hated to just walk away from one of the world's rarest, most spectacular birds, as if I'd won the lottery, shrugged, and returned the ticket. But you can only stare down a monster for so long before it starts to seem tame, and I liked the idea of keeping the memory wild. We had stayed long enough.

Giuiliano, Bianca, and I retraced our steps, high on the Harpy and dopamine, to begin the journey toward the Pantanal and, for me, the rest of the world. On January 30, the Harpy Eagle became one more species on my list — number 657. With the better part of six continents and eleven months remaining, I had a long, long way to go.

6

Gunning It

AT 16,000 FEET of altitude, the ratio of oxygen in the air is almost exactly the same as it is at sea level — about 21 percent — but atmospheric pressure is reduced by half. The low pressure is what upsets your system. When you take a deep breath at 16,000 feet, you're inhaling only half the usual amount of oxygen, so your heart and lungs have to work twice as hard to keep up.

This thought flitted through my hypoxia-addled brain as I gazed down on the country of Peru from Ticlio Pass, high in the Andes Mountains east of Lima, on Valentine's Day, the forty-fifth day of my Big Year. Colorful ridge lines spidered away in pastel shades of red, yellow, and brown, with hardly a scrap of vegetation clinging to the rocks. Lingering snowfields and glaciers dotted surrounding peaks like dirty specks of frosting, and the sky was impenetrably, obscenely blue. The whole riotous scene seemed to be celebrating my good fortune in passing the 1,000 species mark of my Big Year. I had been inching toward this milestone for the past few days, and finally got it with a fluffy Pied-crested Tit-Tyrant. It took twenty-two days to see the first 500 birds of the year and twenty-three more days to add another 500, and I liked the way things were adding up. I laughed, a little too hard, and got a concerned look from Carlos Altamirano, a young Peruvian birder I'd met just a few hours earlier.

"You feel okay?" he asked.

"Never better!" I replied.

In fact, my head ached and my stomach churned indelicately — typical symptoms of mild altitude sickness. At high elevation, the oxygen-starved human body pumps more blood to the brain in an effort to compensate, and those dilated vessels cause the headache. Meanwhile, blood is diverted away from your digestive system, which means the stomach becomes less efficient. I'd landed in Lima, at sea level, less than twenty-four hours earlier, not nearly enough time to acclimate to a change of more than three vertical miles.

Never in my life had I been so high. Ticlio Pass is above the level where skydivers typically jump from planes, higher than most helicopters can safely fly. A rock dropped from this height would fall a third of a mile before striking the summit of Mount Whitney, the tallest mountain in the Lower 48 states. At this spot, I was more than twice as high as any particle of the entire continent of Australia, and I sure felt like it.

Dizziness swept over me as Carlos snapped a picture to mark the occasion.

"Feliz Día de San Valentín!" he said, grinning.

In the photo, I am smiling in front of the Andes Mountains, standing alone with feet shoulder width apart and hands stuffed deep in the pockets of my black down jacket. My shoes and pants are visibly dirty, my hair is sticking up, and binoculars dangle loosely around my neck. Behind me, an empty road snakes around several hairpin bends before disappearing down the mountainside. It is a portrait of a man who, for the past 45 days, has done nothing but look at birds and who, in the back of his mind, knows that he will spend the next 320 days doing nothing but the same.

What I didn't know, at that moment, was just how crazy things were about to get.

✛ - ✛ - ✛

Months earlier, when planning the logistics for South America, I had earmarked a full twenty-one days to cover Peru, a country bigger than the combined areas of Denmark, Italy, Switzerland, Portugal, Romania, the Netherlands, Austria, Hungary, and Poland. For birders, it is an exciting part of the world to visit: you've got everything from desolate coastal deserts to the snow-capped Andes to the Amazon, with all kinds of elevational gradients and tropical diversity in the mix. About 1,900 bird species have been recorded in Peru, of which nearly 150 are endemic — that is, found nowhere else. Compared to the rest of the world, these numbers are staggering; the United States, for instance, has fewer than half as many species in an area eight times as big.

But traveling here can be hazardous, especially off the beaten path. Virtually all foreigners who visit Peru head straight for Machu Picchu, the fifteenth-century Inca city that is now swamped by more than a million tourists each year. It would be nice to see those ruins, but on this trip I had to focus on the birds. Awaiting me were tanagers to chase through the cloud forest, owls to spotlight in the jungle, and hummingbirds — including one very special hummer called the Marvelous Spatuletail — to stalk among the Andean valleys. Three weeks would scarcely be enough to scratch the surface of Peru's bird life, and that's not even considering the difficulties of getting around this country.

Things have improved since the *Sendero Luminoso* ("Shining

Path") period of guerrilla revolt, severe economic turmoil, and political unrest in the 1980s and 1990s, but Peru is still a raw, developing nation. It produces more cocaine than any other country, except possibly Colombia, and has all the trouble that goes with the drug trade. Outside major cities, you're lucky to find pavement. Some regions have no roads at all. In the deep Peruvian Amazon, there are still a couple of native tribes relatively untouched by civilization, including the reclusive Mashco Piro of the Madre de Dios region — an area I planned to visit — who figured in a sensational murder in 2011.

Birds don't stick to tourist traps, of course, so I needed someone local to help navigate this complicated landscape — someone who lived in Peru and understood its culture and birds. I contacted a couple of guides at ecotour companies, but they were less than helpful. Others didn't reply at all. In the end, I realized there was only one man to turn to: the bird-crazy Swede of Peru, the man who, when I mentioned his name to several friends, came across as a modern-day warrior, post-punk rocker, and international birding legend.

His name is Gunnar. It rhymes with "lunar."

I'd heard a few rumors about Gunnar Engblom, and had even come close to meeting him several times, but he was like a ghost, popping up in unexpected places, then disappearing back into Peru. Two months before the beginning of my year, I was at a birdwatching festival in Texas when someone at a party turned to me and said, apropos of nothing, "Did you know that Gunnar Engblom showed up here today but was immediately detained by the authorities?" It was simply assumed that I knew who Gunnar was and that I would want to know that he had been detained by the authorities. I chalked it up to idle cocktail conversation and forgot all about it until months later, when I met Gunnar for the first time. After I asked him about it, the subject morphed into a fascinating story about something else, and I still have no idea what happened at that bird festival in Texas.

Some tales are true, some exaggerated, but everyone in South America seems to know Gunnar. Originally from Sweden, he first traveled to Peru as a thirty-year-old biologist in 1990 — the year that monetary inflation hit 12,000 percent — and returned for several months each year before moving permanently in 1998 to Lima, where he's flourished ever since. He quickly fell in love with the country's birds and began to pursue them with singular zeal, developing a reputation for new discoveries and for bravery in treacherous situations.

Once, in the early days, following patchy information, he took a public bus across the Andes and found himself escorted off by armed guerrillas at a checkpoint. This was serious: two British birders had just been captured and executed by Sendero Luminoso soldiers, their bodies never recovered, and kidnappings were common at the time. Gunnar, crouched on the side of the road, explained that he was broke and just looking for birds.

"They pointed at my binoculars and demanded for me to hand them over," he told me. "But they were nice binoculars, and I didn't want to lose them! So I said no, but they could have my camera, which was basically a piece of crap. I told them it was a really valuable camera and that I'd donate it to the cause as a supporter."

After a lengthy interrogation, the guerrillas became so baffled by this Swedish man's babbling about birds in accented Spanish that they just let him go.

"The best part," Gunnar said, "is that I was wearing a T-shirt that day of Che Guevara" — the Marxist revolutionary instrumental in the Cuban Revolution. "Just imagine!"

These days, insurgency is less worrisome than plain old logistical chaos, which Gunnar confronts with practiced equanimity as he guides visiting birders around the country. Strikes, strandings, accidents, and natural disasters are part of daily life in Peru, but Gunnar is not a man given to panic. He can put together any trip, on any budget, and now runs a full-time business outfitting custom itineraries for birding expeditions.

When I sent him a message to explain my mission, Gunnar replied immediately and enthusiastically.

"I am the right guy to talk to!" he wrote. "I love these kinds of challenges, and am glad to be involved. Time is money for most people. Time is lifers for birders. Count on me for Peru!"

He was as good as his word, and soon drafted a schedule on a shoestring for my proposed dates, encompassing every corner of Peru. Only later did I realize quite how ambitious the itinerary was: Gunnar intended to wring every possible second from our twenty-one days in his adopted country, targeting endemic birds all over the map. This wasn't a regular tour — it was a saturation patrol. He would personally accompany me for most of the trip, and we would rendezvous with local experts in each region. Gunnar also found an American birder from California, Glenn Sibbald, an environmental scientist from Sacramento, who would join us for the full three weeks; Glenn's extra company, cost-sharing, and good humor turned out to be an enormous bonus. All around, it seemed like a great, if potentially exhausting, plan.

And so, after leaving Brazil — the memorable Harpy Eagle with Giuliano and Bianca in the Pantanal, plus another ten days with other excellent birders in Belém/northeastern Brazil and in Itacaré/east-central Brazil — I touched down in Lima with high expectations. When I landed, I found a brief message from Gunnar: "Just back from a successful and disastrous day trip. Lots of good birds. I will meet you in Santa Eulalia Canyon at 5pm."

He had arranged for a local birder to pick me up with a driver, and they waited diligently with a sign at the airport. We did a little birding in urban Lima and then took off out of town. As we ascended toward the 16,000-foot Ticlio Pass that afternoon, one single-lane switchback at a time, my head swam with the altitude and I began to wonder what, exactly, I had gotten myself into.

✦ - ✦ - ✦

As promised, Gunnar met us at a roadside gas station where, after some transfers of people and belongings, he jumped into the driver's seat of our van. Carlos, the birder who had just taken me across Ticlio Pass, sat shotgun while I occupied the back seat with Glenn, who had arrived a few days before. The four of us rolled out.

I was glad to be heading to lower elevations after spending much of the day around Ticlio, though the idea of "lower" was relative. For the first days in Peru, Gunnar had planned an assault on the central highlands for a few key endemic birds. We wouldn't quite reach 16,000 feet again, but the Andean valleys in this region were known for their hardy, high-altitude residents, and we'd sleep a couple of nights above 13,000 feet. My head still ached, and I hoped my system would acclimate quickly.

I had little time to size up my new companion before we hit the road again. Gunnar was in his fifties and had kept the sinewy physique of a long-distance runner — in fact, he was training to run the Boston Marathon in a couple of months, hoping for a competitive time — and he bristled with energy. He sported graying stubble, a gap between his front teeth, and a baseball cap with MORE BIRDS embroidered across the front. I liked him immediately.

"Here's the plan," he said, as the van slalomed around slow-moving trucks, pedestrians, farm animals, and potholes along a cliffside, guardrail-less road. "We're heading for a place called Andamarca and a bird called the Black-spectacled Brushfinch — a super-endemic species, first described to science in 1999, that is known only from a small part of the Cordillera in central Peru. We have a good chance to see one, but Andamarca is kind of far from here." He paused to glance at his watch. "I think we can just make it if we drive into the night, sleep in the van, and then get up at sunrise."

Carlos, Glenn, and I nodded. It was worth a shot. I wouldn't see a Black-spectacled Brushfinch anywhere else.

Gunnar explained that he had spent the past two days scouting with a group of birders and that they'd had some great sightings, but had gotten their vehicle stuck on a remote, muddy road while trying to cross a landslide.

"The spot was so narrow that we couldn't open the doors against the cliff on one side, and there was a sheer drop on the other," he said. "It took us a while to get things sorted out, and we lost a lot of time. But don't worry, we're not going to try that road today — it's been ruled out!"

Instead, we turned off toward the Upper Andamarca Valley and rattled onto a single-lane dirt track hewn into the side of a mountain. Gunnar knew the route and kept his foot down, driving us onward with unstoppable enthusiasm, but as the sun set it became clear that we had a long way to go before reaching the brushfinch stakeout. When darkness descended, a heavy fog settled on the landscape, shrouding everything in black drizzle. The road snuck around sharp bends without signs, folding us ever deeper into the mountains; I had the surreal impression of dramatic scenery in the dark and a gaping void on the downhill side. No other cars passed us and, after a while, I lost all sense of direction. We pressed on for hours into the night until my eyelids drooped, conversation died, and I slumped against my seatbelt.

Finally, just after midnight, Gunnar murmured, "Okay, this is it! The brushfinch spot!" We had entered a precipitous valley covered in cloud forest, though all I could see in the headlights was mud and drizzle. A light rain fell as Gunnar gingerly parked on a wide spot and switched off the engine. There were no lights, no stars, just swirling mist and the vertiginous sense that a couple of feet from our wheels the world dropped into a bottomless abyss. The four of us reclined our seats as far as they would go, closed our eyes, and drifted off after a very long day.

I stirred awake a couple of hours later to the sound of steady rain drumming on the van's roof. Outside, dawn was dissolving into gunmetal skies, and a chill had seeped under my layers of clothing. Gunnar, Carlos, Glenn, and I were each curled up, awkwardly propped in our respective positions, and we awoke with groans and stretches.

"Hey, can we run the heater for a bit?" asked Glenn. "It's freezing in here."

Gunnar grunted from the driver's seat, groped around for the key, and turned it in the ignition. Nothing happened.

"Hmm," he said, after a few seconds of silence. "I think we might have a dead battery." He tried a couple more times, but the van stubbornly would not start.

"Oh well," he said, apparently not too bothered. "We might as well go for the brushfinches now and deal with this later. Dawn is our best shot for finding these birds, and it's already getting light outside. Let's go!"

The four of us eased out of the cramped van and stood for a minute in the rain, stretching, taking in the spacious Andean view. In the moody light, I could better appreciate our position. We had parked next to a ravine where a waterfall gushed across the road surface and abruptly disappeared over the edge of a cliff. Lush, wet forest clung to the mountainside, and through a break in the mist I could see farms scattered far below us on the valley floor. Everything dripped from the rain, which was now slashing down.

BirdLife International lists the Black-spectacled Brushfinch as endangered based on its tiny range and threats of habitat destruction; it is known only from five single localities, and the population seems to be shrinking. It's a neat-looking bird, about the size of a potato, gray and black with orange on the back of its head. On close inspection, it's possible to see a bright white mustache stripe and the namesake black smudge around each eye. These birds prefer damp forest with patchy openings between 8,200 and 11,100 feet elevation. They aren't particularly secretive but they tend to stay inside cover, either scratching on the ground or sitting in bushes, so they can be hard to spot.

Gunnar and Carlos led the way, walking slowly along the road while scanning for movement. A pair of White-capped Dippers foraged energetically for aquatic insects below the waterfall, plopping their plump bodies into fast-rushing water to snag their prey. Scarlet-bellied Mountain-Tanagers, dressed in blood and ink with sapphire accents, streaked across openings like bursts of static electricity. Several types of hummingbird, including a Velvetbreast, Starfrontlet, Metaltail, Sunangel, Violetear, and the exquisitely named Shining Sunbeam, buzzed around colorful flowers, tiny droplets of water glistening on their iridescent feathers.

Locating the brushfinches took more than an hour, by which time I was soaked and shivering. Finally, Carlos pointed out a pair of the birds teed up in a bush, their feathers matted and disheveled but nicely showing the distinctive field marks. After a minute, they disappeared back into the forest, leaving us to exchange damp high-fives for number 1,027. It was a muted celebration, but I was happy that we hadn't come all this way for nothing.

Our attention soon returned to the van, which now stranded with its dead battery between a cliff and the waterfall — no space to try a push start. What to do?

Just then, a little white car appeared around the bend, navigating slowly toward us through the rain and muck — the first vehicle we had seen since the previous day. Gunnar waved and approached, conferred with the driver for a moment, then gave a thumbs-up and a smile.

"These people are going to help us with our dead battery," he said.

The car stopped behind our van, and its driver, a five-foot-tall man with friendly features, got out. The rest of his family stayed put, preferring to keep out of the pouring rain. I counted at least seven bodies sardined inside, squished against the windows; they sat quietly, patiently, and watched us with round, curious eyes.

The man didn't have jumper cables but he did have a screwdriver, which he used to remove the battery from our van. Then he removed the battery from his own car, which he left running, and switched batteries. This had the desired effect: our van started right up, and his little sedan was able to charge the flat battery. He didn't bother to switch them back — "They're the same size!" he said — and cheerfully drove off with his family, leaving us to wonder what might have happened if they hadn't passed by.

The generosity of this man, whose name I never knew, moved me. Time and again during the year, people like this — utter strangers — would generously bail me out of tight situations. Why did they do it? I could be a criminal, for all they knew, yet they noticed a need and took the time to do what they could, be it switching a dead car battery, pushing a van out of the mud, or offering food, transport, or a place to stay. Acts of kindness from strangers continually surprised, buoyed, and humbled me, and just saying thank you never seemed to capture the fullness of my gratitude.

Gunnar got back in the driver's seat.

"Okay, we nailed the brushfinch," he said. "Let's go!"

The exchange had cost us less than an hour, and we were in good spirits despite being soaked through. We left the Andamarca Valley, navigating across an exposed flank of the Andes, with the rain still falling out of a gray sky and birds flitting here, there, and everywhere.

Two days later, Gunnar, Glenn, and I arrived in Huánuco, a city of nearly 200,000 in east-central Peru. Carlos caught a bus to return to his house farther north, with plans to rejoin us in a few days closer to his home territory. Huánuco is said to be a delightful colonial city — "the soul of the Andes, dressed in jungle," according to Peru's tourism board — but I had no time for urban distractions. We rolled into town at 11 p.m. after another long drive on some of the world's most dangerous roads. Then Gunnar announced that we would be leaving again at 2:30 a.m.

I was used to getting up before dawn, but 2:30 was pushing it, especially after several days of very little sleep.

"Gunnar, why not 3:30?" I asked, in a slightly exasperated tone.

He looked sympathetic but wouldn't budge.

"Tomorrow is our Golden-backed Mountain-Tanager quest," he replied, "and we have to be in the elfin forest at dawn. The road up there is pretty sketchy, so we'll need at least two hours to make it."

This point was inarguable — I simply had to see that rare mountain-tanager — and so we checked into a hole-in-the-wall hotel for a couple hours of rest, setting our alarms for a ridiculous hour.

When Glenn and I staggered downstairs at the appointed time, Gunnar was sitting in the lobby with his laptop propped open, making last-minute arrangements on the hotel's Wi-Fi.

"I just booked us a flight back to Lima for this afternoon," he said, in a chipper mood. "That should give us plenty of time to reach the mountain-tanager spot, with extra birding along the way."

I rubbed sleep out of my eyes and thought, this guy is inhuman.

He's booking same-day flights at two in the morning. How does he do it?

We set out in quiet anticipation, leaving the dim streets of Huánuco for a rural track that began to switchback steeply up out of town. As the road climbed past potato fields and open pastures, its condition rapidly deteriorated until Gunnar, in pitch darkness, was navigating around fallen boulders, eroded channels, and sudden drops. Glenn and I bounced in our seats in a state of stoic acceptance, resigning our bodies to whatever might befall us. Driving in Peru, especially at night, is best done with a certain dispassionate attitude, somewhere between nonchalance and apathy.

I tried not to think of the grisly statistics. Broadly speaking, in Peru you are nearly ten times as likely to die in a traffic accident as in the United States. The website TripAdvisor, in an article about how to rent a car in Peru, begins by saying, "It's not a good idea to drive in Peru. Driving in Peru should be considered an 'extreme sport.' The main rule here is that the bigger you are, the less you follow the rules."

The U.S. State Department officially advises against driving in Peru, "particularly at night or alone on rural roads at any time of day," and the British Embassy emphasizes the point: "Driving standards in Peru . . . are poor, with stop signs and traffic lights frequently ignored. Drivers overtake on either side, with little concern for pedestrians or oncoming traffic. Crashes resulting in death or injury take place almost every day."

Bad roads are an unavoidable hazard of traveling in developing countries, especially when trying to access remote birding destinations, and I well knew the risks of spending so much time on them. Several prominent birders have perished in traffic accidents, including the late Phoebe Snetsinger — the first person ever to see 8,000 species of the world's birds — who completed her life list in 1999, when her van rolled off a highway in Madagascar.

Vehicle crashes are the number-one killer of travelers worldwide, far ahead of headline-grabbing terrorist attacks, plane crashes, and epidemics; according to the U.S. State Department's careful records, more than one-third of all Americans who don't make it home are involved in a car, train, or boating accident (a combined 3,104 deaths just between October 2012 and June 2015). And on a global scale, more than 90 percent of all crashes occur in low- to middle-income countries, where infrastructure and safety standards are lacking. Statistically speaking, driving a car — especially in a country like Peru, at night, while sleep deprived — is the most dangerous thing you can do.

Already I'd seen some horrific accidents, including a gasoline tanker that had jackknifed, flipped, and exploded on a highway in central Brazil on the same day I saw the Harpy Eagle. We had passed that stretch of road early in the morning without incident, and then, returning a few hours later, found the blackened, burned-out wreckage blocking traffic in both directions. Apparently its driver had fallen asleep at the wheel, probably at the exact same time that I was enjoying the eagle nearby. "We just have to remove the body," said a guy in an orange vest. "Then we can push the truck off the pavement."

Dwelling on such incidents wouldn't help anything, so I willed myself into composure on these long drives. Deep down, car accidents remained my biggest worry, a fear that would become only too real a few months later in northern Tanzania. But there wasn't much I could do about it, other than digging out long-disused seat belts from all kinds of vehicles. (In Argentina a taxi driver once admonished me, "Oh, you don't need that! I am a very safe driver!") Life always carries risk, and on the road I tried to sit back and enjoy the ride.

After a couple of hours of ascending switchbacks, Gunnar announced with excitement that we were nearing the top of the climb — just in time, because streaks of dawn were beginning to smudge the eastern horizon. The road had become a rough, rocky, muddy, two-wheel track cut into the mountainside, and it finally gave out in a flat, muddy area on a saddle, just below a beautiful patch of elfin cloud forest. As Gunnar initiated a three-point turn to park the van facing downhill, the van's wheels suddenly skidded, spun around, and dug in. We had arrived, and we were stuck.

Glenn jumped out to assess the situation. As he walked around the back of the van, I heard a shout.

"Hey, we seem to be missing something!"

Gunnar reluctantly switched off the engine and we disembarked. In the dim light of dawn, I could see Glenn's silhouette standing behind the van, and I walked back to join him, stepping carefully around muddy spots. He pointed silently. The entire rear bumper assembly was gone, apparently ripped off by a rock during our rough drive in the dark. The van's shape looked funny without it, like a horse without a rump.

No wonder most birders who visit this spot opt to hike the last five miles, I thought — but I couldn't have done that. It wouldn't have left enough time to come up here.

"Well, I guess we'll look for it on the way down," Gunnar said, scratching his head. "And we can push the van out of the mud later, when it gets light. Let's go for the birds first."

Without much discussion, the three of us grabbed our binoculars for the short walk up to the forest. Suddenly, I was glad for the early wakeup: we still had to find this tanager, get the van unstuck, and drive back down the mountain in time to catch an afternoon flight from Huánuco. Thanks to Gunnar's unwillingness to sleep past 2:30, we still had plenty of time.

Golden-backed Mountain-Tanagers have been seen in only a couple of places in central Peru, where the species is restricted to high elevations in the eastern Cordillera. Even apart from its rarity, the bird is a real stunner: vivid yellow and black, with a shining blue cap and fine reddish streaks. Locals call it the *Ave de Oro* — literally, the Golden Bird — and, given a good view, you can't mistake one for anything else. Not many birders have had the chance because it lives in such remote terrain, and I was one of these lucky few.

The Golden-backed Mountain-Tanager also has an interesting history. The first person to describe one for science was the legendary Neotropical bird expert Ted Parker, who is widely regarded to have known more bird vocalizations than any other human (he died in 1993 in Ecuador, in a plane crash, during a bird survey). Parker's report of finding the bird, on his very first trip to South America, was published decades later from handwritten notes, and it's a gripping account of hiking up this same mountain with camping gear. It took him three days to see it, upon which he wrote, "In the early morning light its intense golds, blues, and velvety black colors against the lichen-covered limbs melted in to create a memory that will always be with me." This discovery was one of Parker's first and most lasting ornithological achievements.

Here, I was walking in Parker's footsteps. As Gunnar, Glenn, and I hiked up to 11,500 feet in the cloud forest, my body sensed the thin air; a cool mist rose, and birds started to become active with daylight.

Gradually, our list of sightings grew. A hummingbird called a Blue-mantled Thornbill, flashing its iridescent green and purple gorget, buzzed around some low vegetation next to the trail. Brown-backed Chat-Tyrants, little bigger than poofy Ping-Pong balls, called noisily from exposed perches, and Gunnar spotted a lethargic Barred Fruiteater, patterned in dark shades of green and black, sitting inconspicuously in the canopy. Then a fast-moving flock of small birds swept through, and the pace picked up: Pearled Treerunners and noisy Citrine Warblers joined a brilliant Yellow-scarfed Tanager, endemic to Peru. I almost missed a couple of tiny, drab, brown birds skulking in the undergrowth — the enigmatic Pardusco, a super-local species, known only from these highlands, classified in its own genus.

All of it was marvelous — the fresh air, new birds, beautiful landscape. Even if we didn't find the marquis mountain-tanager, just being in this place was worth the hassle. On top of the eastern Cordillera, in the mists of the cloud forest, the bustle of Peru's chaotic cities felt very far away.

The trail crested a ridge and dipped down the other side, plunging into a steep set of switchbacks. Gunnar bushwhacked confidently across a meadow to stay high, traversing at right angles to the trail, until we reached an isolated stand of gnarled, wind-sculpted trees. The vegetation here was stunted in the face of harsh elements, just above tree line — hence the name "elfin" forest. This was the realm of the Golden-backed Mountain-Tanager, and Gunnar, Glenn, and I settled in to wait.

I was prepared for a long vigil, but this morning the birding gods decided otherwise. I'd been standing quietly for less than ten minutes, overlooking the patch of trees, when Gunnar whisper-shouted: "There, right below you! In the big tree at three o'clock!"

Sure enough, something moved within the foliage and hopped into plain sight. Even with my naked eye, the black-and-yellow body was strikingly obvious, and through binoculars the view was simply magnificent: I could see the bird's little blue cap and even the fine red streaks on its underparts as it foraged from limb to limb, at one point approaching close enough for a photo op. We watched for several minutes in complete silence, each enjoying the experience on his own terms. For me, the combination of rarity, good looks, inaccessibility, and beautiful surroundings would rate this Golden-backed Mountain-Tanager, species number 1,112, as one of the best sightings of the year.

We lingered for a while, sifting through other birds in the area, before calling it a morning. As always, I could practically hear the clock ticking, and we had a long journey to reach Lima by evening. Someday, I thought, it would be nice to return here with a little more time to explore and relax — a feeling that was starting to seem familiar during my travels.

Three weeks is a criminally short amount of time to spend birding in Peru, and this abbreviated timeframe meant that I was rushed at every stop, always running from one place to the next without any rest. Might as well get used to it. I still had to cover the northern part of the country, the Amazon, the white sand forests near Iquitos, and the southeast, not to mention the rest of South America and the wide world.

First, though, our stuck van had to be extricated. When we walked out of the forest an hour later, Gunnar climbed confidently into the driver's seat while Glenn and I positioned ourselves at the bumperless back end to push.

"I hope this doesn't spray mud all over us," I said, "or we won't be very popular when we get to the airport."

But when Gunnar turned the key, the engine wouldn't start. He leaned out the window and smiled.

"Guys, I think we have another dead battery!"

Our van must have developed some kind of electrical problem that drained off the power. This was worrying, especially on a remote mountaintop.

Then I walked around the passenger side and noticed something else: both right tires were flat! Rock punctures hissed from the front and back, and we had only one spare.

"Uh," I said, "I don't think we're driving out of here."

We stood for a moment and contemplated the situation: stuck in the mud with a missing bumper, a dead battery, and two flat tires, in the middle of nowhere, with a flight to catch in a couple of hours.

What to do?

"We start walking," Gunnar said.

The three of us gathered our things — I picked up my back-pack, Glenn carried a more unwieldy suitcase, and Gunnar had two big bags, one in each hand — and started briskly hiking down the mountain, unsure what lay ahead.

At least a few birds were around. We paused to admire a Many-striped Canastero singing from a tuft of grass, its streaky brown-and-white plumage blending in with the habitat. A little farther down, a Red-crested Cotinga watched us pass. But I was anxious; hiking all the way down this road would take all day if we couldn't find help, and then we'd miss our flight out of Huánuco. All I could think about was the wasted hours, the missed flight, the lost birds.

"Maybe we'll find our bumper," Glenn said.

In the clear light of day, I could see just how rough this road was that we'd ascended in the dark; jagged rocks and potholes presented a fearsome surface even to walk on. We had been lucky to make it to the top and see the Golden-backed Mountain-Tanager before running into trouble.

After a couple of miles with no signs of civilization, the three of us rounded a corner to discover about a dozen Quechua farm-ers sitting in the shade, eating potatoes for lunch. Most were kids, and they looked up with the expressions one might expect upon the sudden appearance of three gringos heading toward them with air-port luggage — kind of like, say, a meteorite flying into their potato field.

Gunnar didn't miss a beat.

"*Hola,*" he said, walking right into the group. "*Alguien quiere una naranja?*"

He set down his bags and zipped one open to show that it was completely stuffed with dozens of fresh, ripe oranges, and he started handing them out. The kids' expressions changed from surprise to delight: it wasn't a meteorite that had crashed into their midst, it was a fruit stand.

"Gunnar, were you going to carry those oranges all the way down the mountain?" asked Glenn, looking incredulous.

We had bought a large bag of them at a roadside stall a couple of days ago, and I'd been wondering what Gunnar meant to do with the fruit, as he had way too many for us to eat. They must have weighed twenty-five pounds.

"You never know when a few oranges will come in handy!" said Gunnar, looking pleased.

The farmers invited us to join them for lunch. We sat down and ate boiled potatoes and oranges while they stared at us, whispering to each other and giggling. I could imagine that this visit would provide entertainment long after we had gone. The potatoes were delicious.

After a while, Gunnar explained our predicament and pointed to several dirt bikes parked nearby. Could we get a ride down the hill? This request sparked a fresh round of giggles, but soon enough three kids volunteered to take us far enough for a taxi transfer. Our bags were carefully tied to the dirt bikes and we climbed on, two to a saddle.

My driver was a quiet seventeen-year-old named Rolando who had seven siblings and lived next to a potato field. I rode right behind him, crotch to crotch. On a dirt bike, there is no such thing as personal space — it was common in Peru to see four or five bodies zooming past on one motorcycle — and I wasn't sure of the etiquette. Would it be weird if I clasped him around the waist, or should I rest my hands on his shoulders, or maybe try something else? In the end, I grabbed the seat on either side of my thighs and hung on tight, trying not to lean too far when we banked around corners.

He politely asked why I was visiting the area and I tried to explain, in broken Spanish, that I was traveling around the world for an entire year just to look at birds. It's a big project, I said, to set a world record. I love birds: *me encantan los aves.* Birds are amazing, I added, for clarity.

Stone silence.

Sometimes, and this seemed to be one of them, my adventure existed so far beyond the bounds of a person's everyday life that it simply could not be comprehended. I ran into this reaction repeatedly, especially in very rural areas. A few weeks later in Guatemala, for instance, I tried the same explanation on a local indigenous girl and said that I'd started the year in Antarctica. After a few seconds, she replied, earnestly, "Is that in Guatemala City?" But this can happen anywhere, and it's not always worth getting into the full story. Just before this Big Year, when I had my last haircut in the United States, at a regular salon on a Wednesday, the hairdresser asked brightly if I had the day off work. What should I say — that I was about to set off on an obsessive, forty-one-country world tour of birdwatching, hence the need to shave all extraneous hair? Sure, I replied. Just running a few errands.

At the bottom of the mountain, we hopped off the bikes and said our *muchas gracias* while Gunnar tipped the kids a few Peruvian soles for their help. They buzzed off, looking happy to head home. Gunnar then ordered a taxi by cell phone, describing in detail which dirt road to take, and called some other poor soul to go deal with our injured, abandoned van. Soon enough we were on our way to the tiny Huánuco airport, with barely enough time to catch the afternoon flight back to Lima.

When we finally arrived at the open-air check-in counter, tired and dusty and sweaty and hungry, there was some confusion. I couldn't figure out why the ticket agent wouldn't hand us our boarding passes; she talked too fast for me to catch the drift. It was only when Gunnar stepped in, with his usual calm in the face of trying circumstances, that I understood.

"Our flight has been canceled," he said. "The plane didn't make it in today. We might as well have stayed on that mountain."

+ – + – +

Then I got sick.

It happened a couple of days after our antics in the highlands. That canceled flight meant spending a night in a hotel without electricity, then a ten-hour drive to Lima the following day, where Glenn and I arrived at the Jorge Chávez International Airport exactly eighteen minutes before our connecting flight to Chiclayo took off. We sprinted through security and just made it, sinking low into our seats to avoid the glares of other passengers. Meanwhile, Gunnar stayed home in Lima, planning to fly up and join us the following day, and Carlos — the young Peruvian birder from Ticlio Pass — met Glenn and me when we landed up north.

Here was the plan: Carlos, Glenn, and I would begin an ambitious west-to-east transect across northern Peru, a diverse region with several hundred possible bird species. Most organized birding trips dedicate about two weeks to this route, but we had scheduled just six days for the whole shebang, which gave little room for error. Gunnar would join us for some sections. We even had a driver, Julio Benites, who could handle the long days and cook meals in the field.

I had visited this region once before, a few years earlier, so I knew many of the birds and places already — the first familiar ground since Argentina, weeks ago. My most-wanted bird here was the Marvelous Spatuletail, a spectacular hummingbird with peculiar tail streamers that is found only in one remote valley. I hoped to rack up a lot of species, as each day we'd be in completely new territory.

Things started well. On the first day in northern Peru I added thirty-seven new species, including some nice "Tumbesian" birds native to the dry, coastal plain shared by Peru and Ecuador. At a place called Chaparrí Reserve, a community-run conservation project east of Chiclayo, local birder Juan Julca kindly pointed out Tumbes Sparrows, Tumbes Tyrants, and a dapper-looking Elegant Crescentchest skulking through the scrubby woodland. Then we stayed up after dark to search for Peruvian Screech-Owls and Scrub Nightjars by spotlight.

That evening, though, it was difficult to write my daily blog entry — a task I never failed to do, no matter how long the day had been. "Edging on hallucinatory sleep deprivation," I noted. "Maybe that will help me see more birds?"

I'd now been in Peru for a full week and had averaged less than four hours of sleep each night, without any chance to catch up. Gunnar had driven us hard, wanting to reach every possible species in our allotted time. I appreciated the effort but wondered how long I could take this grueling schedule — it was physically wearing me down and I was having trouble concentrating. I was becoming a pro at power naps, even while sitting upright.

The next day I hit the wall.

It was probably inevitable. Carlos, Glenn, Julio, and I stopped at a place called Abra Porcuya for a picnic lunch, along a rural road with good access to foothill forest. All of a sudden, even though it was a warm, sunny day, I started shivering and couldn't quit. My throat hurt, and I had the dizzy feeling that if I didn't sit down, I'd vomit.

Carlos spotted a bird called a Piura Chat-Tyrant and I lifted my binoculars, but my arms were shaky. I knelt down on the roadside and tried not to think about my queasy stomach.

"I don't think I can keep walking," I mumbled.

Glenn suggested we abort the afternoon's plans and proceed

straight into Jaén, the next town. At first I protested, but it was no use — my system had decided to force the issue, and now I had a fever. Julio pulled up the van, I climbed in and reclined my seat, and we drove onward in silence.

It should have been a two-hour trip, but halfway to Jaén, traffic was backed up on the two-lane road, apparently because of an obstruction ahead. Julio didn't hesitate: he pulled into the opposing lane and zoomed past more than a mile of parked cars until we reached the scene of an accident, where a bus had collided with a tractor on a blind curve.

"I have a sick person and we are going to the hospital!" Julio yelled at the people directing traffic. (We were, in fact, going to a hotel.)

When the flipped tractor was cleared, we rocketed ahead of the jam on a blessedly traffic-free road.

In the next few miles, I couldn't help but notice two large billboards placed by the Jaén health ministry along the highway which said, in large letters, *"Cuidado . . . ¡El Dengue es Mortal!"* — "Be Careful, Dengue Fever Is Deadly!" The billboards featured a picture of a mosquito on a red drop of blood and were written in a dramatic font suitable for a horror movie.

When you have just contracted a mysterious fever, signs like this are not encouraging. Sprawled in my seat, I wondered what I was in for. I hoped that it wasn't dengue — which often manifests as severe joint pain, hence the disease's nickname, "breakbone fever" — but it was too early to tell. Dengue fever is serious in tropical areas around the world, especially in South and Central America; hundreds of millions of people are infected with dengue by mosquitoes each year, and the incidence is growing, which is why even on the hottest, most humid days I covered myself in clothing that I had treated with mosquito-repelling pyrethrin.

Dengue was just one of a suite of tropical diseases on my radar in 2015. Before leaving home, I had read up on all of them. Chikungunya, another mosquito-borne virus, first introduced to the Americas in 2013, had infected more than a million people in the Caribbean region by the end of 2014; like dengue, chikungunya usually presents a painful fever and has no specific treatment or vaccine. Malaria kills up to a million people each year, mostly in Africa, and I'd packed a supply of antimalarial pills that I would start taking each day later in the year to ward that off. Leishmaniasis is really creepy, caused by a flesh-eating parasite spread by sandflies, and I actually knew someone with a large, open wound to show for it. Chagas disease can lead to sudden heart failure ten to thirty years after being transmitted by the bite of a tiny, blood-sucking "kissing bug"; more than eight million people are probably infected with Chagas, though most Americans have never even heard of it. The West African Ebola outbreak of 2014–2015 had fewer than 30,000 total cases (and 12,000 deaths) — a blip by comparison — but I was worried about Ebola, too, as I was headed to the African continent in a few short months.

On the plus side, I figured I didn't have yellow fever, because I had been immunized against it. And I probably didn't have tetanus, diphtheria, or pertussis — potentially life-threatening bacterial diseases — because I had gotten a Tdap vaccine, along with a polio booster, a flu shot, and a hepatitis A vaccine, in one ghastly pre–Big Year medical visit that ended with me, and my lifelong blood-injection-injury phobia, in a dead faint. I had to be revived by three nurses with smelling salts.

It's easy, when you're far from home, to panic when you get sick, and I tried my best to keep calm. After all, the likelihood of contracting a scary disease is small compared to many other things that could go wrong. I had come down with a flu, that was all, and I tried not to think of all the diseases described as having "flu-like symptoms."

When we reached the town of Jaén, Carlos's phone rang. It was Gunnar, calling from Lima to check on our progress. He had been planning to fly up and join us that afternoon but said he'd missed his flight because of heavy traffic, so he would try to catch us the next day.

Carlos handed me the phone.

"Hey Gunnar, I'm not feeling well," I said.

"How bad is it?" he asked. "Did you see a Henna-hooded Foliage-Gleaner?"

"No," I said. "I really need to lie down now."

"Always got to be one of those days," he said, philosophically. "Listen, you still have time to try for a few birds near Jaén this afternoon. I know a great spot. Just head out by the Utcubamba River —"

"Gunnar, I can't talk now," I said, suddenly violently dizzy and nauseated.

I hung up and handed the phone back to Carlos.

"You should rest," he said, looking concerned. "Are you sure you don't want to go to the hospital? You're very pale."

"I just need to lie down for a while," I said. "I'm sure it will be fine."

We checked into a hotel, where I splurged on an air-conditioned room all to myself.

"I don't want to keep you up with coughing and all that," I explained to Glenn. Mostly I just wanted to be alone. Despite my efforts to keep calm, I was already wallowing in self-pity.

Once sealed in my room, I jacked up the AC, curled into the fetal position on the center of the bed, shut my eyes, and tried to dismiss the feeling of having been run over by a garbage truck. Chills came in waves, shaking my body, which ached from head to toe. The emotions came pouring out, too; I suddenly felt wretchedly homesick, lonely, and scared. Several times I crawled into the bathroom on all fours but couldn't throw up. Sweat soaked the sheets, leaving me shivering uncontrollably under a mountain of soggy covers. Making matters worse, I felt vaguely guilty for being so miserable, because when you are living the dream, as I clearly was, you are supposed to be happy. The hours ticked slowly by.

My fever lasted well into the night. Carlos and Glenn checked in a few times, but otherwise I lay immobile for hour upon hour, thinking dark thoughts. I had been pushing hard without a break since the beginning of the year, with early starts and late nights almost every day. My system had maxed out. Glenn and I had talked about it a couple of days ago, and his words came back to me now.

"A lot of people assume it's a sprint," he said, "but nobody can sprint hard for an entire year. That's crazy. Your year of birding is more like an endurance event, and it's not even a marathon. It's more of an ultramarathon, so long and complicated that it's impossible to reach the finish line without approaching it in sections. You can't peak too early; you have to pace yourself."

Now, sacked out and staring at the ceiling, Glenn's point struck me hard. I'd finished several marathons in past years, enough to understand the importance of pacing. Professional athletes know that world distance records are usually set with negative splits — in other words, the second half of a race is run faster than the first half — and I supposed that this Big Year might be just the same. Expending too much energy during the first couple of months could set an unsustainable pace. It was still only February and I had a long way to go, the equivalent of being just four miles into a 26.2-mile marathon. Yet I could already feel the exhaustion setting in after so many long days without rest. Perhaps getting the flu was my body's way of telling me to cut it some slack.

With my energy at its lowest ebb, one bright thought came shining through: I knew for certain that I would not quit. My main worry from the start had been the possibility of getting burned out on my favorite activity. Now my sagging spirits were soothed somewhat by the sharp realization that burning out was not going to be a problem. If I could remain enthusiastic during the worst moments, then I could be sure that birding wouldn't get stale. My sense of purpose was still strong. I just had to believe that my body would bounce back. Really, the most frustrating part of getting sick was that it kept me from looking for birds.

The following morning, I wobbled downstairs with binoculars ready. Carlos stood by the front desk and looked up with surprise.

"What are you doing up?" he asked. "You look terrible."

"Yeah, but I'll feel a lot better if we can find some birds today," I said, with a half smile.

I'd been in bed for eighteen painful hours and hadn't eaten anything in more than a day, but the fever had broken and I could stand up without vomiting. Might as well go birding.

Carlos tried to dissuade me, but then, surprisingly, Gunnar walked into the room — apparently he had managed to catch a late flight from Lima and had arrived during the night.

"Ready to rock?" he asked, grinning broadly.

"Let's go find a spatuletail!" I answered.

Our posse trundled out of Jaén, a little worse for wear but glad to be on the road again. If anything, I was now more committed: a case of the flu only made me want to see more birds.

The Marvelous Spatuletail spot was another two days' drive eastward, and by the time we arrived there I was feeling well enough to walk in the forest. I had a hacking cough that threatened to break my ribs, but a course of Azithromycin was helping with that, and as long as I could function enough to continue birding, the quest was on.

We parked at the Huembo Reserve, near the town of Pomacochas in the Utcubamba Valley — the only valley where you can reliably find a Marvelous Spatuletail — late in the afternoon. Huembo is a conservation success story, a ninety-six-acre sanctuary set up by the American Bird Conservancy and the Asociación Ecosistemas Andinos (a Peruvian conservation organization) as an easement with the local community; a small shade-grown coffee plantation supplements entrance fees to protect the land from deforestation. Several feeders are always kept full of nectar for hummingbirds, and some benches have been arranged for birders to sit on while waiting for the star of the show to appear.

This particular star is worth biding time for. Even without its bizarre tail feathers, a male Marvelous Spatuletail is unmistakable: tiny, fierce-looking, with a spiky purple crest, green throat, and a flashy black line down the center of its body. But it's the bird's tail that sets it dramatically apart, earning it the distinction of "world's most spectacular hummingbird." (Practically all of the world's 342 species of hummers are gorgeous, so tread lightly with such super-latives — but this one has my vote.)

Uniquely in the bird universe, spatuletails are born with only four individual tail feathers: A pair of stiff, pointy feathers in the center, flanked by two wildly elongated, curved shafts that cross over each other to end in round, shiny blue paddles. The effect is like two butterflies fluttering behind the bird's body, each one moving independently of the bird itself. When it gets excited, a male spatuletail can whip these paddles back and forth over its head in a frenzied display, waving them like semaphores to attract the attention of a nearby female. (You can't make this stuff up; check out the videos on YouTube.) Otherwise, he seems content to carry his strange tail around like a miniature turbocharged peacock.

As with the Golden-backed Mountain-Tanager, this bird is both stunning and rare — a knockout combination. Marvelous Spatuletails are restricted to the eastern slope of one remote valley in northern Peru, occur in low numbers, and are thought to be declining; the species' total population is estimated at fewer than 1,000 individuals. At the Huembo Reserve, Gunnar, Carlos,

Glenn, and I sat down on a bench to watch dozens of humming-birds, of ten species, swarm like bees around several sugar-water feeders. The sight was mesmerizing.

"Bronzy Inca," Gunnar said, when an unusually drab hummer darted in for a sip.

"Long-tailed Sylph!" exclaimed Carlos, gesturing toward a hummingbird with shimmering tail feathers longer than its own body.

"Ooh, and a woodstar," I said, pointing out one that flew like a bumblebee. "Maybe a White-bellied?"

"*Sí*," Carlos confirmed. "Good call!"

So many hummingbirds surrounded us that they demanded full attention, and after nearly an hour I realized that I was completely captivated — for the first time in three days, I had forgotten all about the flu. These hummingbirds were as good as a swarm of antibodies.

It's amazing, I reflected, what we will do for our passions, and what our passions will do for us. At home I might still have been flat in bed, but here I was in remote Peru, barely even aware that my body was out of whack. The crisp mountain air, good company, and onslaught of birds offered a healing combination, and the real star hadn't even materialized yet.

I was beginning to wonder if he'd keep his appointment when the male Marvelous Spatuletail, species number 1,235, zipped out of nowhere, briefly lit on a twig to scan the scene, and moved in aggressively for his turn at the feeder. The effect was like a rock star stepping onstage. His little tail paddles bobbed along behind, floating like a twin escort of pea-sized helicopters while he slurped down sugar water. Light scattered from his iridescent head and throat patches, sending neon beams of green and violet into space. When you're so small and quick, predators aren't a big worry, and this bird flaunted himself like he owned the forest.

"Dang," Glenn said. "That is some crazy, crazy bird."

It is impossible to put into words what washed over me just then: euphoria, transcendence, a sense of things coming together. I was ecstatic and pensive, filled with adrenaline. The hummingbird was magnificent, but its allure owed as much to desire as beauty. Because I had spent so many years scrutinizing this bird in books and magazines, it almost didn't seem real in three dimensions.

There is something metaphysical about the human connection with nature, and we each find our own points of contact. For me, that afternoon, the Marvelous Spatuletail represented something far beyond a single bird. It distilled the whole experience of Peru, incarnated in avian form — all of the rough, raw material of an entire country compressed into one bright and shining diamond.

I spent two more weeks with Gunnar and crew, continuing to have adventures and misadventures. On a single day in Manú National Park, we survived two major landslides, a broken transmission, a flat tire, and a lost driver's license, and twice had to be towed out of the mud before an agricultural workers' strike completely shut down the road. We suffered torrential rain in the Amazon, endured the aftermath of a bus accident in the highlands, and briefly got lost in the forest one evening as darkness fell. I developed a bacterial lung infection that persisted for weeks afterward, despite two courses of antibiotics, and I couldn't ever catch enough sleep.

And just when we thought that was it, Peru had one last surprise. Immediately after Gunnar dropped me at the airport, he was mugged at a stoplight in Lima while sitting inside a taxi on the way home, and lost all of his birding gear.

"All of a sudden there was a violent sound and the crash of glass splattered all over the back seat of the cab," he recalled. "Before I realized what was happening, a dark-clad man reached in the window and grabbed my backpack containing practically all my working material. I was stunned."

In that instant, Gunnar lost both his cameras and telephoto lens, laptop, iPad, and GPS, among other things — particularly devastating because of the three years' worth of photos on the computer's hard drive. I felt terrible about the robbery. It was an awful way to end three wild weeks of birding.

"In Peru it is best to count on things not going as you hope and be happy when they do," once quipped John O'Neill, an acclaimed ornithologist and artist who has discovered more than a dozen species of birds within Peru since the early 1960s. That's the nature of traveling in such a rough and beautiful country: you take the ups with the downs.

Gunnar likes to reference O'Neill's quote when things take unexpected turns.

"The gods know I have learnt that lesson after years of living in Peru," he said. "I never get worked up or get despair in these situations. Eventually things work out with some patience. Stay flexible and reassess the situation."

Whatever Peru cost us in wear and tear it more than paid back in birds. By the end of our twenty-one days, I had recorded 784 species in the country, more than I would see in any other nation during the year. Of those, 488 were new additions, and 242 turned out to be unique — not seen anywhere else. I left Peru with 1,468 birds on the year list, amped up by a huge boost in sightings. It could not have been done without the help of generous Peruvians and the unflappable genius of Gunnar Engblom.

7

An Angel of Peace

LATE AT NIGHT, while waiting at Lima's spacious Jorge Chávez International Airport for the plane to Ecuador, I remembered something Gunnar had mentioned a few days earlier. A young Dutch birder had announced his intention to spend 2016 birding around the world, and Gunnar was curious about my reaction. This was the first I'd heard of it. I had been so focused on strategizing my Big Year, and then so busy traveling off-grid during the Big Year itself, that I didn't know anything about it. Now, sitting quietly at the gate, I pulled out my laptop and snooped around.

From what I could tell, Gunnar was right: a man named Arjan Dwarshuis was indeed plotting a round-the-world birdwatching trip the following year. He seemed to live in Amsterdam and to spend most of his time out birding — he was almost the same age as me, just four months younger — and he had posted a map on his personal website, with an itinerary spanning about twenty countries. In Africa and the United States he'd arranged long road trips, and in various places he apparently had convinced friends and family to join him. It sounded like fun, though I didn't think he could reach his goal of 5,000 species of birds with the route he had chosen. He appeared to be in it for the experience, and I hoped we might run into each other. It would be like meeting my Dutch twin.

I'd always assumed that someone would come along and challenge any mark I set, even if this guy didn't do it. For me, finding 5,000 birds was the game, but the real adventure was in the people I would meet, the places I would visit, and the stories and memories I would accumulate along the way. The third month into my Big Year, I wasn't thinking too hard about the world record anyway, which was still thousands of birds away and months in the future, even if I got that far. Still, it was unsettling to imagine that the very instant I finished my own year, someone else would embark on a global tour and conceivably challenge my record. What if he was inspired by my quest to up his game? After all, he'd have the benefit of my successes and failures, like following a blueprint, and he could alter his strategy to squeeze out more birds.

Slightly annoyed, I shut my laptop. Then, annoyed at feeling annoyed — what was this, a competition? — I boarded the plane, flew to Ecuador, and forgot, for the moment, all about it.

Ah, Ecuador: home of the Incas, fried guinea pigs, the world's highest capital city, the farthest point from the center of the Earth, and, acre for acre, the highest biodiversity of any country — all within an area smaller than the state of Colorado.

For birds, Ecuador offers nothing short of a tropical paradise. Virtually every habitat is represented, from coastal deserts to snow-capped peaks to the Amazon basin, and more than 1,700 species have been recorded — 16 percent of the world's birds on less than 0.0006 percent of its land surface. For birders, conditions are just as alluring: unlike neighboring Peru or Colombia, Ecuador has a long history of conservation, is relatively stable and safe, has a well-developed infrastructure, and is small enough to cover efficiently. If you want to see the most species of birds in the shortest amount of time, Ecuador is without doubt the best place to do it.

The importance of natural diversity in this tiny nation cannot be overstated. It's even written in the constitution: Ecuador is the only country in the world to recognize "Rights of Nature" — the idea that ecosystems have inalienable rights, just like people do — at the highest legal level. "Nature, or Pachamama, where life is reproduced and occurs, has the right to integral respect for its existence," states Article 71 of the country's constitution, in accordance with the Ecuadorian concept of *Buen Vivir*, which emphasizes harmony with other people and nature above material development.

This constitution was passed in 2008 following the election of Rafael Correa, a former economics professor who campaigned for president on a popular socialist platform. It didn't stop Correa from auctioning 12,000 square miles of Amazon rainforest to Chinese oil companies in 2013, or from overturning a ban on the sale of shark fins, but at least he pays attention to the environment. I once bumped into him, almost literally, when he visited the Galápagos Islands before being sworn into office during the fall of 2006. I was there on a study abroad program with the university where he used to work. He looked at me and said, "I used to teach here, but now I'm the elected president!" Correa remains the only national president I've ever met in person, for better or worse.

After the nonstop intensity of Peru, Quito felt immediately friendly and familiar. In past years I had spent about eight months in Ecuador, on three separate trips — more than any other country outside the United States — and now I looked forward to revisiting some old haunts and familiar birds.

It was pleasant, for a change, to arrive in a place where I didn't feel overwhelmed by everyday details. The constant exposure to new destinations in Peru often gave me the impression of wandering through a museum, and, more than two months into this adventure, I was beginning to worry that my sense of discovery would dull into complacency before I reached the end of the world. New discoveries make us feel good, but we sometimes forget that the main prerequisite for novelty is ignorance — and it's no fun to be oblivious all the time. One of the biggest risks of moving too fast is that you always stay a beginner, and I wanted to dig deeper than that, to soak everything in and keep advancing. Time was an unaffordable luxury while racing from place to place, which meant that I sometimes felt like a blind sprinter. The best antidote was familiarity: because I had spent time in Ecuador before, I knew what to expect here, which meant I could settle in and focus on the real highlights.

My plane touched down at Mariscal Sucre International Airport at two in the morning. By dawn, I was in the cool, misty, high-altitude cloud forest at Yanacocha Reserve, above the city of Quito, with a local birder named Manuel Sánchez. I remembered this spot from my first, mind-boggling trip to South America with a group of young American birders in 2005. I returned to Ecuador in 2006 for the university study abroad program, which included three months in the Galápagos, and came back in 2012 to spend a season at the remote Tiputini Biodiversity Station in Amazonian Ecuador tracking Wedge-billed Woodcreepers with radio telemetry.

This time around, I wouldn't be visiting the Galápagos — too far, for too few species — but instead planned a quick assault on the most diverse parts of Ecuador: the northwest cloud forests, the Andean slopes, and the Amazon lowlands. You could spend a lifetime in these areas without seeing every bird, but I had little more than a week to track down as many species as possible, helped by several locals who thoroughly knew the territory.

Manuel and I wandered slowly down the trail at Yanacocha, enjoying the cool air near 11,000 feet and the forest birds. Hummingbirds stole the show, highlighted by an iconic Sword-billed Hummingbird perched in the mist. Although I'd already seen one in Peru, I took a few minutes to admire this individual as it, in turn, admired us from the safety of its high vantage. The Sword-bill has such a long bill — adapted for probing certain tubular, hanging flowers — that it must preen itself with its feet and usually holds its head upright to rest, like someone who is balancing a javelin on the tip of their nose. No other bird has a bill exceeding its own body length; I snapped a few photos of the distinctive silhouette. Other hummingbirds, including a shimmering Golden-breasted Puffleg and a dazzling little Rainbow-bearded Thornbill, species numbers 1,478 and 1,479, lured us farther down the trail.

As we walked, Manuel, who wore glasses, a scruffy beard, a plaid shirt, and a warm coat, talked passionately about conservation. A native Ecuadorian, he had studied science communication at Edinburgh University before returning to Quito to guide ornithologists and work in ecotourism, and he was only a couple of years older than me. Like me, Manuel decided to pursue birding full-time, and believes that watching birds is a powerful tool for sustainable development. He is part of a new generation of Latin American conservationists who are working hard to preserve nature by getting people inspired about their birds. It's a tough career path, but Ecuador — with all its natural riches and constitutional commitment to the environment — presents a better chance than most places. And Manuel isn't the only one to take advantage.

"Have you heard of Ángel Paz?" I asked, as an Andean Pygmy-Owl called in the distance.

Manuel stopped and looked as if I'd just asked a question so utterly obvious it almost didn't bear answering.

"Of course," he said, speaking slowly. "All the birders in Ecuador know him. That guy is an absolute legend."

A few years ago, reports began to surface of a man in rural Ecuador who, improbably, had figured out a way to attract antpittas — which belong to one of the skulkiest and trickiest families of birds in the New World. Taxonomists recognize about fifty species of antpittas, collectively limited to South and Central America. All of them are plump, long-legged, short-tailed, and upright-standing, shaped like eggs on legs, and they are secretive. Most of the time, antpittas hop on the ground within thick vegetation; the conventional way to see one is to listen for its call and then try to sneak up on it. Birders love them and dread them in equal measure.

The largest of the family is the Giant Antpitta, an enigmatic species that stands up to eleven inches tall and weighs ten ounces. Despite its size, the Giant Antpitta is despairingly difficult to observe. It lives only in primary cloud forest with dense understory and is known from just a few scattered locations in Ecuador and Colombia. Nobody knows its population (the best estimate is a couple thousand individuals), its nesting cycle, or exactly what it eats. It's a spectacular bird, for those lucky enough to catch a glimpse: salmon orange with fine black barring, a bluish cap, long legs, and large, watery, inky black eyes.

The man who first befriended the Giant Antpitta is Ángel Paz — literally, "Angel of Peace" — and his story is as unusual as his name. In a former life, about a decade ago, this particular Ángel worked as a logger in northwest Ecuador. His father purchased a beautiful tract of cloud forest on a flank of the Andes, and Ángel moved in to start chain sawing.

"The faster you cut down trees, the more money you make," he told me with some pride. "I used to be one of the fastest tree cutters in this region."

The forest on his property hosts a display site, known as a lek, of an iconic and easy-to-see bird, the Andean Cock-of-the-rock — neon orange with black wings and a fluffy crest. The birds gather at the lek each morning so that females can view the males' elaborate courtship rituals and magnificent plumage. About a decade ago, someone advised Ángel to charge tourists admission to view the birds. He built a trail to the spot and, sure enough, people paid to see the spectacle. Ángel decided to leave the trees alone in that part of the forest.

One day, while Ángel was walking with a birdwatching group on his trail, a plump creature hopped out of the undergrowth and turned its dark eyes on the visitors, who promptly freaked out.

"That's a Giant Antpitta!" one exclaimed.

After everybody calmed down, they told Ángel: "Forget the cock-of-the-rocks. If you can show this bird to birders, they will pay double."

Ángel had seen the bird before but didn't think much of it. In fact, the bird sometimes followed him around when he was cutting trees, apparently attracted by disturbed grubs, and wasn't particularly shy, though it usually stuck to dense cover. Ángel called it Maria, an endearing local name for many types of small birds in Latin America. He began to methodically stalk Maria, trying to figure out her habits.

He offered the bird food, unsure what it might like to eat. He started with pieces of spaghetti and meat, but Maria didn't have a taste for human delicacies. So he scrounged around for worms, and, lo and behold, the bird gobbled them down. He began bringing fresh worms to the same spot each morning so that Maria would get used to the gifts, and eventually he trained Maria to come when he called.

At the time, most birders would have scoffed at the idea of hand-feeding a wild Giant Antpitta. Books emphasized the species' secretive and elusive nature (rightly so), and few people imagined that one could be habituated to handouts. But Ángel didn't read birding books; he was a logger who saw an opportunity to make a little extra cash. Maybe, looking back on it, the idea of feeding an antpitta wasn't that far-fetched, as antpittas have been known to shadow large mammals inside the forest, apparently to scavenge disturbed insects.

When word got out, amazed birders began showing up to see for themselves, and Maria's fame quickly spread. It seemed too good to be true: a species that had traditionally been regarded as near-mythical was suddenly real and viewable — guaranteed even — within a couple of hours' drive of Quito.

Soon, so many people were visiting Ángel that he quit logging, planted a few blackberry crops, and spent his time hanging out with birds and birders. He found that he could make a better living by leaving the forest intact than by cutting it down; as long as the birds stuck around, he'd have a steady income from entrance fees. Gradually he learned about the other species on his property and became an expert in showing them to visitors. He put up fruit and hummingbird feeders, constructed new trails, and, each morning, kept his worm-feeding appointment with Maria.

I arrived at Ángel's property, along with another Ecuadorian birder, Edison Buenaño, four days after leaving Manuel at Yanacocha. Edison and I had connected after I took a quick trip to eastern Ecuador for some Amazon specialties, during which I had gotten thoroughly rained on. As we parked in front of Ángel's house in the cloud forest, I reveled in the anticipation of what was sure to be a standout morning.

Ángel stepped into his driveway to greet us as Edison and I hopped out. He was dressed in pastel greens with a camouflage

down vest over a khaki shirt, a military green baseball cap, and binoculars around his neck. He smiled warmly.

"Bienvenidos a Refugio Paz de las Aves!" he said.

Without much chitchat, the three of us headed straight into the
forest. Ángel took us first to where it had all started: the Andean
Cock-of-the-rock lek. I'd seen these birds before but couldn't pass
up the opportunity to watch their displays at close range. Just after dawn, we walked quietly along Ángel's trail to the spot where
male cock-of-the-rocks postured, hopped, bobbed, and contorted
in a mesmerizing combination of color, motion, and sound. As
their grunts and squawks filled the air, I marveled at how these
birds had been returning to the exact same tree for many years.
Cock-of-the-rocks are polygamous; the gorgeous males compete
for the attention of passing females, and after mating, the females
fly off to build a nest and raise their chicks alone. The birds use lek
sites like this one for generations, as long as they remain undis-
turbed.

After a few minutes, I realized that I was alone with the birds —
Edison and Ángel had slipped away. Completely transfixed, I stayed
put to watch the cock-of-the-rocks in full swing. A male perched in
front of me, snapped his bill, flapped his wings, arched his back,
bowed deeply, croaked, bobbed his head, did several pushup-like
maneuvers, and crowed in my face. Even within the understory of
this dense forest, in the muted light of dawn, his electric orange
feathers glowed like a fluffy, misshapen light bulb, and he made
a popping noise to signal the start of each display. It was all very
flattering to me, but a few seconds later I noticed that this bird
had higher hopes: a maroon-colored female sat inconspicuously in
a tangle of foliage, watching intently as the action unfolded. Two
other males danced nearby, seemingly trying to outdo each other's
moves. If a female likes what she sees, she'll land next to a male and

peck his neck and they'll mate on the spot, but this one didn't seem impressed by any of them. She flew off a minute later.

Just then, I heard a different sound.

"Psst! Noah — over here!" whisper-shouted Edison.

I turned around to see him gesturing from a patch of foliage inside a small, lush ravine.

"Come, very quietly!" he called.

Leaving the cocks, I tiptoed down. As I approached, trying not to slip on the slick mud and sopping vegetation, I could see Ángel standing behind Edison, staring at something on the ground.

"It's not an antpitta," Edison said, "but look at this! Ángel is feeding a family of Dark-backed Wood-Quail!"

Sure enough, several chunky, grapefruit-sized birds were pecking at the ground, almost at Ángel's feet, partially hidden by damp leaves. He tossed something in their direction, and one of them immediately gulped it down.

"A bite of banana," Edison said. "These wood-quail don't like worms."

Ángel looked up and smiled.

"*Sí?*" he said.

"*Sí, sí, sí!*" I replied, hardly believing my luck.

Wood-quail are as infuriatingly cagey as antpittas, and I never expected to see one here. Evidently Ángel had expanded his hand-feeding operations. Chalk up a nice bonus for the Big Year.

"Okay," said Edison, translating for Ángel, who speaks no English. "Let's keep moving — we still have to see Maria. This was just the warmup."

We retraced our steps to take a different trail, this time switch-backing sharply uphill. The path was covered by damp leaves, but Ángel had maintained it well, leveling its surface against the slope and placing stairs on the steepest sections. We tunneled through thick, damp brush in a dim understory where little light penetrated. The forest dripped from fog and mist, the only noises the muted calls of distant birds.

Walking in a cloud forest is a hushed experience, almost like hiking through a landscape of freshly fallen snow. The foliage absorbs sound, wraps you in its embrace, and dampens conversation. As we approached the antpitta spot, nobody spoke; except for my own breath, I was struck by how profoundly quiet this place was.

The calm was shattered by Ángel, who stopped us above a switchback, surrounded on all sides by tangled undergrowth. Without warning, he cupped his hands around his mouth, took a deep breath, and shouted at the top of his voice: *"MARIA! MARIA! VENGA VENGA VENGA!"*

I was so startled that I almost lost the significance of this moment. A few seconds later, a plump bird hopped placidly into the open, stood on the path a few feet in front of us, and cocked its head expectantly.

"Hola, Maria!" said Ángel, looking pleased.

"The famous Giant Antpitta!" said Edison, like a sports commentator.

"Holy moly," I said.

Ángel opened a container he'd been carrying in his pocket, reached in, grasped a juicy earthworm between two fingers, and expertly flicked it at the bird's feet. Maria stared at us for a moment with big, black eyes, then bent over, pecked up the worm, and swallowed it whole.

Ángel tossed several more worms and Maria ate them all with clinical efficiency. The bird was so close that I could see its toenails, the tiny hook on the tip of its beak, and the bristly orange feathers at the base of its forehead. It seemed unafraid, expectant, perhaps a bit curious, though I had difficulty reading any expression into its shadowy eyes. Who knew what this bird thought of us? There was no telling, and once the worms were done, the show was clearly over. Maria took one last glance at us, hopped back into the vegetation, and disappeared.

"Wow!" I said. "That was incredible!"

In two minutes, I'd snapped dozens of photos of Maria posing on the trail, in three-quarter profile with one leg half bent, like a model showing off her best angle. It was the closest encounter I'd ever had with any antpitta, and this one happened to be the rarest. It hardly seemed fair to count as only one more species for the year (number 1,607).

"*Gracias,* Ángel," I said, at a loss for words.

"Oh, we're not done yet," said Edison, with a knowing nod.

Our *tête-à-tête* with the celebrity now over, we continued along the trail where, in short order, Ángel showed us five additional species of antpitta: Chestnut-crowned, Yellow-breasted, Ochre-breasted, Moustached, and Scaled. The first three quickly hopped in for worms, just like Maria had. The Moustached was too shy to come close — still in training — and the Scaled, apparently having already eaten its breakfast, preferred to sit on a branch and sing at us.

It was like I'd arrived in heaven, suddenly finding myself in a celestial forest made of clouds, with an Ángel who called rare, colorful birds out of the bushes left and right. Maybe, I reflected, as we retraced our steps for a hearty late breakfast cooked by Ángel's wife, this was closer to a fairy tale than a religious experience. Ángel was a real-world prince of the forest, communicating with its shyest animals. My impression was solidified when he casually pointed out a roosting Lyre-tailed Nightjar, a pair of roosting Rufous-bellied Nighthawks, a Rufous-breasted Antthrush, and an Olivaceous Piha along the path.

Ángel has named some of his favorite birds: besides Maria, there's Andrea the Chestnut-crowned Antpitta, Esmeralda the Yellow-breasted Antpitta, and Shakira the Ochre-breasted Antpitta, a tiny creature with a peculiar habit of twitching its chest from side to side.

For Ángel, too, the whole thing must seem rather like a fairy tale. Once upon a time the woodcutter set out to cut down his forest, but now he is richer than he could ever have imagined, precisely because he left the trees intact. His property hosts more than 2,000 birders each year, all hoping to see the antpittas, and everyone pays an entrance fee. When Edison and I visited, Ángel had just finished construction of a beautiful new house, with extra rooms for birders upstairs, decorated with hand-carved antpitta artwork and surrounded by lush plantings of flowers. From the balcony you can overlook most of his property: a few blackberry fields backdropped by a solid green canopy of cloud forest, stretching all the way to the horizon. In this place of life and warmth, I wondered why anyone should desire more.

It's a fantastic true story, one of the best examples of small-scale conservation success I'd ever seen. The worm-feeding idea has spread, too; in recent years, others have started promoting antpitta attractions in Colombia, Peru, and elsewhere in South America, channeling even more ecotourism dollars into local habitat preservation.

Ángel doesn't even have to advertise. He's so busy that advance reservations are necessary to secure a place on the daily tour. When he discovered his wings, Ángel found his life's work. Every morning, even if nobody shows up — a rare occurrence these days — Ángel Paz walks into the forest with a can of worms, cups his hands around his mouth, and greets the bird that changed his world.

"Maria! Maria! Venga venga venga!"

8

Flying Free

As MARCH PASSED into April, a restless urge to fly north swept over me. Millions of migratory birds in the Neotropics — hawks, sandpipers, warblers, grosbeaks, tanagers, orioles — were now on the move, beginning their grand annual migration across the hemispheres, and I could sense their haste to chase the spring.

Ornithologists have a special word for the migratory instinct of birds: "Zugunruhe." It comes from the German words *Zug* (move, migration) and *Unruhe* (restlessness, anxiety), and it is mostly an academic term — used in somewhat-obscure scholarly works such as "Zugunruhe Activity in Castrated Bramblings," published in the journal *IBIS* in 1961. Researchers have shown, under controlled conditions, that caged songbirds try to hop, flap, and jump in the same compass direction as they would naturally migrate. Birds become visibly restless during migration season, changing their patterns of sleep and physical activity. In other words, birds are programmed to move.

Poetically, spring is the season of renewal — a

cleansing of winter with the promise of a brighter life ahead. Birds hustle north in the spring, covering ground twice as quickly as when they make the return trip in the fall, as if they can't wait to reach summer. Migrants of any species go for the same reasons — territory, mating, and food — and so, evolutionarily speaking, long-distance travel is the ticket for better living.

Migration is one of the great wonders of the bird world, having been remarked upon since the days of Homer, who wrote that cranes disappeared to battle Pygmies at the far end of the Earth, and Aristotle, who believed, among other things, that redstarts turn into robins during winter. The reality, that more than half of North American bird species fly long distances twice each year, is even stranger than these fictions, and birds continue to surprise us. Researchers still haven't resolved how migration evolved: Did temperate birds fly south, or was it tropical species that went north? And modern tracking technology has revolutionized our notion of how birds connect far-flung parts of the globe. Scientists recently discovered that Bar-tailed Godwits nesting in Alaska fly directly to their wintering grounds in New Zealand, taking a mere nine days to complete the 7,500-mile one-way trip without ever stopping to rest.

With spring arriving in the Northern Hemisphere, it was time for me to migrate, too. During the first part of the year, I had stayed within South America, from Argentina to Colombia. Now I felt the magnetic pull of Zugunruhe. On April 13, after 103 days and 1,977 species of birds in South America, I left the continent in a contrail and headed north. Central America sits at the midsection of a geographic hourglass, funneling birds on the wing, and I was swept into this flow like a leaf in a stream.

This was no time to rest. I spent three weeks tracking down the birds of Colombia with a sharp group of local birders, then put in a solid five days with an awesome guide named Guido Berguido in Panama, where I hit the number 2,000 milestone with a male

Shining Honeycreeper. After a strategic one-day foray into Jamaica with some research friends to see their endemic birds, I landed in Costa Rica, where I met local birders Roy Orozco and Johan Fernández in the capital city of San José. Here would be my main chance to pick up a wide variety of Central American species, and I was stoked to explore the country with these new friends.

I'd connected with Roy through BirdingPal. When I asked if he might like to spend a week with me in Costa Rica, he responded with thoughtful enthusiasm.

"I will be happy to help you," he said. "This could be an opportunity for a new big experience, and the chance to make a new friend who shares the same passion as I do."

In the same message, he sketched out a rough itinerary and suggested that his bird-obsessed friend Johan might join us for the week.

"We can be flexible," Roy wrote, "and stay wherever we end up each evening. Instead of reserving rooms in lodges, we'll look for little places in towns where the three of us can sleep for about $30 per night. Each day we can plan the next move over dinner, following a general route."

The plan couldn't have suited me better. Costa Rica, bordering both Atlantic and Pacific Oceans and squeezed between North and South America, sits at a crossroads of bird distributions; in one day you can visit dry forests, cool mountains, and tropical jungles. Long-distance migrants flood through each spring and fall, boosting local bird populations, and many spend their winters here. About nine hundred avian species have been recorded within Costa Rica's borders, an impressive diversity for a country less than half the size of Tennessee.

Costa Rica is also an extraordinarily nice place to visit, especially if you're keen on the natural world. I fell for this country years ago, during four invigorating months of banding birds at different sites operated by the Costa Rica Bird Observatories. The locals, calling themselves *ticos*, are friendly and laid back; their standard greeting, *pura vida*, means "pure life," and it is as much a philosophy as a way of saying hello.

No other Latin American nation, and perhaps no country anywhere, has done more to promote an environmentally friendly image. In 1949, following a civil war that left few people happy, Costa Rica constitutionally abolished its army — an unprecedented move at that time for any nation — and redirected all military spending toward health care, education, and environmental protection. This bold move marked the beginning of a strong economic rise, and today the country leads Latin America in health and education indicators. Life expectancy is now longer than in the United States. For years, Costa Rica's citizens have ranked number one in both the Happy Planet Index and the World Database of Happiness. Nearly 25 percent of the land is protected in reserves and national parks (by percentage, the world's highest conservation rate), and Costa Rica has more trees per capita, and per square mile, than any other nation. In the past thirty years, the amount of forested land here has, unbelievably, increased — in fact, it has more than doubled since the 1980s — thanks to tree planting and other anti-deforestation measures, partly financed by a tax on gasoline. The national government has pledged to become the world's first carbon-neutral country, and, as of 2015, Costa Rica was 81 percent of the way there.

Taken with a plate of *gallo pinto* (stir-fried beans and rice) and a dash of the ubiquitous Lizano sauce, all of these things combine for a unique and delightful cultural experience. No wonder tourism is Costa Rica's largest international trade, earning more than coffee, banana, and pineapple exports combined. Two and a half million foreigners entered the country in 2015, about one tourist for every two residents, and more than half of those visits were eco-based.

Costa Rica's modern economy would wither without the national parks; it's a win-win for business and for conservation.

Roy, Johan, and I headed straight out of town. Roy had his sights set on a mountain called Cerro de la Muerte to search for highland birds in the isolated Talamanca Range. Despite its name (which translates as the "Summit of Death," for the perilous crossing before the Inter-American Highway was built), this area teems with life: dozens of endemic birds occupy the Talamanca highlands, from the Fiery-throated Hummingbird to the Volcano Junco, and Cerro de la Muerte offers the most convenient access to them.

As we left the city, I got acquainted with my new companions. Roy, thirty-five years old, originally from the town of Quesada in north-central Costa Rica, had graduated as a natural history tour guide. Johan, thirty-one years old, studied natural resource management and discovered his passion for birds while guiding tours. Both of them lived with their young families near Manuel Antonio National Park on the Pacific Coast and took great pleasure in showing the local birdlife to visitors.

"Do you think we'll see a quetzal?" I asked.

Johan laughed.

"Everybody wants a quetzal," he said. "Yes, we have a good chance at Cerro de la Muerte."

"Excellent," I said. "Because you can't go to Costa Rica without seeing a Resplendent Quetzal!"

The scenery became greener and steeper as the highway rose into lush forest, and the air cooled noticeably. For every 1,000-foot gain in elevation, the temperature drops by more than three degrees Fahrenheit; climb 5,000 feet and suddenly it's fifteen or twenty degrees colder. By the time we'd reached the turnoff for Cerro de la Muerte, at nearly 11,000 feet, we were cloaked in a chilly drizzle.

It had taken just an hour and a half to reach this spot from downtown San José, and I marveled at how quickly we had ascended into a completely different world. How many urbanites ever ventured up here? On my travels, I am consistently amazed at how easy it is to access splendid natural places from most large cities, and yet how few people take advantage. Drive an hour or two in any direction from almost any city center, in any country, and you can reach real, remote nature with hardly a soul around.

Roy directed us onto a side road where he thought we'd have a shot at a Timberline Wren — an obscure, diminutive member of the wren family at home in the mountaintops of eastern Costa Rica and western Panama. We stopped at a wide spot and the three of us climbed out into fresh, misty air.

Birds twittered unseen from the cloud forest. It proved to be quite a challenge spotting anything in that heavy vegetation, but gradually we teased out sightings. A curious Yellow-thighed Finch (number 2,180), jet black, flashed patches of neon-yellow feathers from its upper legs as if wearing miniature, fluffy shorts, then ducked for cover. A pair of Black-and-yellow Silky-Flycatchers (number 2,182), patterned in the same colors as the finch, flitted through the canopy. Nearby, a teensy Volcano Hummingbird (number 2,189) perched like a gemstone on a flowering bromeliad, catching the light with its purple gorget. A jeweler might say the hummer weighed twelve carats — a costly gem fit for royalty — but here it entertained us for free.

Johan bounded confidently ahead, calling out names and moving quickly. His face was round and friendly, with short stubble on the chin and thin sideburns. He wore khaki pants and a long-sleeved field shirt, and his binoculars hung from a loose shoulder harness, dangling almost to his waist. When he smiled, his eyes squinted into tiny smiles of their own, and his whole being radiated with cheerfulness.

Roy was quieter, more methodical and more thoughtful. He often stopped to inspect some tiny detail, perhaps on a frog or a leaf, and he observed birds with kindness and patience. He seemed to know every species of creature in the forest and was interested in all of their interactions — not just their names, but how each one fit into the bigger picture. I noticed that Roy walked slowly, paused frequently, and breathed with more difficulty than the altitude might warrant, but he didn't mention it. His body was thin and angular, bundled in warm clothes that hung loosely.

Johan found the Timberline Wren within a few minutes, directing our gaze to a perky brown bird clambering in the undergrowth. A close look revealed its stubby tail, cinnamon brown back, and characteristic white eyebrow, which separated this wren from the similar, more widespread Ochraceous Wren at lower elevations. It was impossibly cute, and I watched it quietly with Roy for a few minutes until a peripheral flash of green distracted my attention.

"Hey, I'm just going to check something out," I said, and jogged off in the direction of the movement.

I could have sworn I'd glimpsed another bird — a bright green one. Around the next curve in the road, a noisy flock of Sooty-capped Chlorospingus worked through the midcanopy, but I ignored these commoners. I got that feeling, almost by instinct, of picking up something unusual in my field of vision, and now I scanned the forest with a sense of anticipation. The chlorospingus flock disappeared after a couple of minutes and I stood alone, wondering what else lurked nearby. With Johan and Roy out of sight around the bend, I didn't want to stay too long and risk missing some goodies.

A few slow heartbeats passed. Then, like a mirage in slow motion, a glistening-green creature detached itself from its green surroundings and fluttered to an open branch in front of me. It banked as it landed, giving a perfect view: this bird had a red belly, white under the tail, black wings, and a small yellow beak. The rest of its body was emerald and jade, subtly iridescent in the cloudy light, with a metallic golden sheen. A fluffy crest covered its head, and long green feathers drooped over the wings like frilly shirt-sleeves. But the most striking feature was the tail (technically, the uppertail coverts), which stretched almost three feet, dangling like a soft, bright green train below the bird's body.

"I've got a quetzal!" I shouted, and Roy and Johan appeared around the corner, relief evident on their faces. We would have had a tough time missing this bird in Costa Rica, and they were glad to nail it down so soon.

The Resplendent Quetzal is Central America's most famous bird, found from western Panama to southern Mexico. It's not particularly rare, but to see one you must spend time in the mountains between 5,000 and 10,000 feet, where the quetzal inhabits mature cloud forests with plenty of fruiting trees. The male is spectacular — "the most beautiful, all things considered, that I have ever seen," once wrote the legendary ornithologist Alexander Skutch — and was traditionally worshiped by the Aztecs and Maya, who associated the bird with the snake god Quetzalcoatl. Today, it is the national bird of Guatemala and namesake of Guatemalan currency, the "quetzal," and you can find quetzals in many places throughout Central America. Because so many tourists visit Costa Rica, with its easy access to national parks, the Resplendent Quetzal has become particularly representative of Costa Rica's highland forests.

As I watched, the quetzal flew a short distance and retreated into a tree cavity. A second later, its head emerged to spy on us, with the tip of its tail still sticking out of the hole.

"It's on a nest!" I said.

"Wow," Johan said. "Wow, wow, wow!"

Roy watched in silence, soaking in the details. He knew this bird very well from long study. His attention didn't waver as he observed the quetzal's behavior, and his manner conveyed contentment.

"The female must be around here somewhere," he said. "They both incubate the eggs, usually one or two in the nest. She might be foraging on wild avocado fruits nearby."

A few minutes later, the quetzal pulled his head inside the cavity, leaving only the end of his tail visible.

"The tail is so long that they have to wrap it around themselves and dangle it out the entrance," Roy said, "or else they risk damaging the feathers."

I tried to imagine what it would be like to carry around something like that — an extra, inescapable part of the body that must constantly get in the way, but that also makes life more interesting and beautiful. Did the quetzal sometimes wish he could cut his tail loose, and just be a normal bird?

Standing next to me, Roy looked as if he could read my thoughts. All of us carry our own burdens, of course, even if they're not always as obvious as the tail of a quetzal.

+ – + – +

That evening at our hostel, I opened my laptop, found an anemic Wi-Fi network connection, and settled down to catch up on email. Top priority was to confirm arrangements with my local contact in Guatemala, where I would land in a few days.

By now I was used to staying connected on the road. Maintaining my online *Birding Without Borders* blog was the toughest part. Every day, I wrote a new entry and, using some of the wimpiest Internet signals on the planet, contrived to send the text and a selection of photographs to my editors. The National Audubon Society hosted these updates on their website and posted each entry as quickly as possible, with an updated species list, map of my travels, and accompanying photos, so that people could follow my progress. Despite the rigors of blogging after long and exhausting days of birding, I never tired of having this amazing connection with the world, and I usually managed to find adequate Wi-Fi somewhere — at hotels, airports, restaurants, and even gas stations.

Using a combination of email, text messages, WhatsApp, Facebook, and Skype — mostly from my phone (with an international voice and data plan) and often while on the road in a car, taxi, or bus — I kept in touch with upcoming birding partners as well as family and friends. Though I spent a lot of time in remote places, I passed through civilization to get from one birding spot to the next, so I wasn't exactly lost in the wilderness.

Even so, as the year unfolded, I was increasingly glad to have made most arrangements before starting out, as it would have been nearly impossible to plan and coordinate everything along the way. When I hit the road at the beginning of January, I carried a spreadsheet with dates, itineraries, and local contacts for every country I planned to visit during the entire year — as well as a detailed flight itinerary and a wad of plane tickets, which I had purchased with the expert help of an agency, AirTreks, that specializes in round-the-world travel. Some details would change en route, and I could be flexible, but planning ahead meant that I was able to stay focused on birding without stressing over the logistics.

At regular intervals, I tried to check in ahead of time with the birders at the next destination so that all would be ready when I arrived, but that wasn't always possible. Some of my contacts spent as much time on the road as I did. Others barely had Internet access and replied to my messages weeks or months after I sent them. My system of birding with locals required a certain leap of faith: once I'd made plans with people, I just had to trust that they'd show up at the appointed time and place. A couple of birders had to cancel for personal reasons, but I expected that; what I couldn't get over was just how smoothly things were going so far.

Now I had a funny feeling that something was wrong with my guy in Guatemala. I hadn't heard from him in a while, which seemed a little odd because I'd be landing there the following week. I wasn't seriously worried because I knew he was one of the best birders in the country and often led tours for visitors. Months ago we'd hashed out an itinerary including Tikal and the highlands, and I looked forward to our five days together.

His name was Hugo Enríquez. I was particularly excited to meet Hugo because I'd interviewed him in 2011 for a regular feature in *Birding* magazine, where I work as associate editor. He was suggested as an interviewee by the magazine's editor, Ted Floyd, who had run into him on a trip in Guatemala.

"Hugo is at the vanguard of a fascinating new development in birding," Ted told me, "namely, the emergence of outstanding local guides in great birding destinations in Latin America."

That was enough for me. I got in touch right away.

We did the interview by email, and the final product ran several pages, presenting a personal account about bird conservation in Guatemala, from tourism to science and research, including the plight of the Resplendent Quetzal, which is threatened by habitat loss. Among *Birding* interviews, this one stood out. Because the magazine focuses on North America, only three out of more than fifty interviewees over the years have lived outside the United States and Canada. Hugo's perspective, as a young and brilliant birder in a country where birding presented a relatively new pursuit, was different and fascinating.

I felt I knew Hugo, even though I had never met him in person. So when I planned a stop in Guatemala during my Big Year, four years later, he was first on my list.

"That would be great going out to the field with you!" he had replied immediately. "Let me know everything you need."

In a few messages back and forth, Hugo had drafted a plan for us to fly to Tikal, spend a day birding there, and drive back to Guatemala City via some highland sites with several key endemics. We would stand a good chance of finding a Horned Guan, one of Central America's most elusive and oddest-looking birds, and we'd see some amazing scenery. I inked him in, booked plane tickets into Guatemala, and moved on to other logistical hurdles. It would be a thrill for me to finally have the chance to meet Hugo after corresponding with him for several years. In birding, this sort of thing happens all the time — you can connect via the Internet with like-minded souls all over the world and then wait a long time for a face-to-face encounter.

Now the situation had become urgent. With our meeting just a few days away, I hadn't heard from Hugo in months. I sent him a message: "Let me know how to meet you when I arrive. Will you pick me up at the airport?"

As I continued through my inbox, the lack of contact and my imminent arrival in Guatemala kept nagging at me, and I decided to try to find another way to reach Hugo. I opened a browser window and Googled his name.

It took a minute to process what appeared. The first result of my search was a recent post from the *10,000 Birds* blog, which often covered news of interest to bird fanatics. The post was titled, "Requiem for a Bird Guide."

"Oh my God," I said, in a tone that made Roy and Johan look up sharply.

With a sense of unreality, I started reading.

"We've lost a truly great bird guide," the post began. "Hugo Haroldo Enriquez Toledo has died, apparently as a result of injuries suffered in an automobile accident."

The walls suddenly closed in. Everything within me and around me seemed to stop. The article offered few details except that Hugo was survived by his wife and six-month-old son, and that the accident had happened a few months ago. As the news sank in, chills ran through me. No wonder he hadn't returned my recent emails. How could I have missed this?

"That's the guy you were going birding with in Guatemala?" asked Johan, looking over my shoulder.

"Yes," I said, blankly. "I sort of knew him, but we'd never met in person."

Roy, Johan, and I stared at each other, unsure what to say. Neither of them had known Hugo. In a weird way, I felt embarrassed — realizing that the man I had been pestering about a birding trip next week had lost his life months ago. I'd been so caught up in South American birds that I hadn't checked the news, and now I wasn't sure if I would have found out anyway.

When people die unexpectedly, they can't say goodbye to every friend and acquaintance. The family tells those who need to know, and from there the news goes out like a puddle on a hot day: it slowly seeps into deep cracks and then evaporates, leaving just the memory behind.

That night, I couldn't sleep. Hugo's accident was terrible; learning about it after all this time only made it worse, and I felt bad worrying about my upcoming trip. What if I hadn't Googled his name? I imagined landing in Guatemala City, expecting to see him there, only to find nobody waiting. And what else was I missing? This year I had consciously decided to put life on hold while I chased birds around the world, assuming that everything else could wait. As the clock ticked during my Big Year, was it right to ignore everything else?

For me, birding is part of life, not separate from it. I know Hugo felt that way, too, because when I interviewed him for the magazine, I asked him about the qualities of an ideal birder.

"The best local bird guide is a friend, fellow, and field partner," he said. "A person with patience and joy."

Those are words to live by. By all accounts, Hugo was a kind, generous, and passionate part of our planet. I regret that I missed my chance to meet him. His death reminded me of how quickly life can disappear, and how precious few are our days on Earth. If anything good can come from the passing of a friend, it is the renewed appreciation for those still with us — and the deeper resolve to live every day with purpose, patience, and joy. May Hugo Enríquez rest in peace.

✦ – ✦ – ✦

Roy woke me up early to see a unique bird spectacle.

"Let's go," he said, quietly. "Johan is sleeping in today, but you and I have an appointment to keep before breakfast."

The three of us were staying at Rancho Naturalista, one of Costa Rica's oldest and best-known birding lodges. We'd arrived late the previous evening after several hours of searching for nocturnal birds on the flanks of a nearby volcano. Johan scored lovely views of a Bare-shanked Screech-Owl with his spotlight, but by the time we reached the lodge, had a quick dinner, and sacked out, it was past 1 a.m. Now, feeling hung-over after a long night of owling, I struggled out of bed and followed Roy into the predawn darkness.

We didn't go very far. A hundred yards from our room, Roy pointed at what looked like a billboard in the forest surrounded by benches. Closer inspection revealed a vertical white piece of cloth, several feet across, tacked to a wooden frame with a roof to keep it from getting wet. Floodlights on each side illuminated the cloth, which glared bright white in the dark forest.

"What is this, an interpretive sign?" I asked. "It's totally blank."

Roy smiled.

"It's a moth trap."

The cloth was liberally covered with insects: bees, wasps, flies, beetles, and other creatures of the night crept around its surface in a macabre horror show. Among them were moths of all sizes, shapes, textures, and colors, some as big as my hand. A few of the moths had gorgeous and intricate patterns, like fancy butterflies, and I spent a while snapping photos of the prettiest ones. The diversity was huge; some mimicked thorns and leaves, others were bright green and blue, and still others had huge, sweeping antennae like little aliens.

"They are drawn to the lights," Roy explained.

"Like a moth to a flame," I said, automatically.

Was it worth getting up early just to see some moths? Most of these were drab, brown, buggy-looking, perhaps scientifically undescribed. There are 10,365 species of birds in the world and nearly 20,000 butterflies, but moths are a black hole — scientists estimate 160,000 species worldwide, and many don't have names yet. Moth identification often requires microscopic examination of their genitalia and barcoding their mitochondrial DNA, and even then it's sometimes impossible to tell species apart. Moth experts are a different breed.

"Just wait," Roy said, reading my thoughts. "The show hasn't started yet."

We settled on a bench to wait for dawn. Gradually, as the sky lightened from black to gray, birds began to stir and call from the surrounding forest; I heard the distant croaking of a Keel-billed Toucan, then the spaced-out notes of a Scaly-breasted Wren tuning up nearby. As soon as enough light penetrated the understory to see shapes and movement, I realized that birds were materializing all around us, and the whole setup suddenly made sense.

"They're coming to eat the moths!" I said. "This is all for the birds, isn't it?"

Roy grinned.

"It's a different kind of bird feeder," he said.

The party kicked off at sunrise: a pair of burly Red-throated

Ant-Tanagers darted in low, their dark red feathers almost invisible in the undergrowth, and perched next to the illuminated cloth. Each one grabbed a fat moth, retreated a safe distance, and efficiently dismembered its breakfast. Then a White-breasted Wood-Wren, no bigger than a golf ball, moved in to snatch a brown moth, and a Canada Warbler appeared, its white eye-ring and flitty movements giving it a surprised, nervous air. The warbler delicately picked off an insect next to the lights and flew off with it.

When a Brown Jay showed up, the other birds scattered. The jay hardly hesitated as it confidently approached the cloth, scanned the menu, and chose the largest, most beautiful moth in sight.

"Not that one!" I cried — it was one of the pretty moths I'd photographed earlier — but the jay was hungry. It seized the fist-sized insect with one foot, pinned it to a branch, and used its beak to rip off the wings, which fluttered to the ground like colorful shrapnel. The moth's body was too big to consume at once, so the jay ate it with fastidious bites.

I watched, spellbound, as birds lined up for their turns. A Bright-rumped Attila, streaky brown with a devilishly red eye and fearsomely hooked beak, snapped up a moth and flung it apart, sending scales flying in every direction. Then a Yellow-bellied Flycatcher seized an insect in midair, and I reflected that this bird, weighing less than half an ounce, would soon migrate several thousand miles to seek a mate and nest in the boreal forest of Canada. It needed all the fat it could store to make the journey.

Roy was scanning intently, and I asked if he was looking for anything in particular.

"*Sí*," he replied slowly, but before he could elaborate, his eyes lit up. "There!" he said, pointing underneath the moth feeder. "You see that small flycatcher? Not the Yellow-bellied . . . Yes! It just hopped onto the branch. Do you see it?"

I focused my binoculars on a plump little bird with a gray head, stubby beak, and ochre-colored underparts.

"Yeah," I said. "Got it."

Roy looked extremely pleased.

"Tawny-chested Flycatcher," he said. "That's the bird I was most hoping to see here this morning. It's a range-restricted species. Very nice!"

Like the other smaller birds, the Tawny-chested waited for larger patrons to eat before making its move. It perched quietly in the shadows, which afforded us great views. Then, in a flash, it swooped toward the white cloth, snatched a moth, and vanished into the forest.

"It comes most mornings," Roy said, "but you never know. Some days, maybe it sleeps in, like Johan. I'm glad the flycatcher was hungry today — now we can go have our own breakfast."

The action died out after the dawn rush, and Roy and I meandered over to the lodge's open-air terrace to meet Johan. Breakfast was served on a colorfully striped tablecloth: fresh orange juice, pancakes with strawberry syrup, a variety of fruits, fried eggs, coffee, and bread. As we sat down, I kept my eye on several sugar-water feeders around the terrace that were thronged by hummingbirds — White-necked Jacobins, Green-breasted Mangos, and Rufous-tailed Hummingbirds. Whether you prefer insects, pancakes, or nectar, I thought, everyone must eat breakfast.

We were joined by Lisa Erb, the longtime manager of Rancho Naturalista, who knew all about my Big Year.

"Did you get the flycatcher?" she asked.

"Yes!" Roy and I said in unison.

Lisa beamed. "Good!" she said. "Maybe later we can go find a Sunbittern, but first enjoy the food. It's all fresh and local."

I was glad to meet Lisa, who has been a fixture of the Costa

Rican birding community since her parents opened the lodge in the mid-1980s. At that time, specialized lodges hardly existed, but she had a vision for a birder-friendly accommodation in the Caribbean hills. Rancho Naturalista has flourished over the years and now includes more than a dozen cozy rooms, giving birders easy access to surrounding mid-elevation forest. Lisa, who wears long blonde hair and cowboy boots, is a perpetual bundle of energy; when not discussing birds, she's apt to gush about horses, food, and local events with a sharp sense of humor.

"Did you see Roy's paintings?" Lisa asked.

"No," I said. "He didn't mention them."

I looked at Roy, who gave a self-conscious smile.

"Well, we have two," said Lisa, who stood up and beckoned me to step inside the main room of the lodge.

"Here's a King Vulture," she said, proudly, "and over there is a pair of Scarlet Macaws."

The framed paintings were luscious oils on canvas in a hyper-realistic style.

"Wow, I had no idea he was such a serious artist!" I said.

The King Vulture perched facing away, its wings spread to catch the sun, while the macaws were depicted in a misty forest. The details of each were executed almost photographically, with a naturalist's attention to plumage and structure, but the compositions had a balanced, painterly feel.

"He paints a lot of birds, wildlife, and Costa Rican images," Lisa explained. "We're lucky to have these two pieces."

With that, she excused herself and I returned to finish breakfast with Johan and Roy. We were in no rush to leave this relaxing spot. I felt a great sense of contentedness — Lisa and her friends had carved out a little slice of Eden here.

"Roy, when did you get so good at painting?" I asked. "Those pictures in there are incredible."

"*Gracias*," Roy said. "I've always liked to draw. Painting is part of my appreciation of the world, I guess."

Johan caught my eye as if there was something more, but didn't say anything. The three of us sat for a luxurious half-hour, mostly without speaking, drinking in the scene.

This year, I was learning to treasure these moments, when the world stopped turning for an ever-so-brief rest. My hectic birding pace meant that I rarely had time to take a deep breath. Somehow, the busier your calendar, the faster it goes; it seemed like only yesterday that I'd been sipping champagne on a ship in Antarctica, but the year was already almost a third over. Not for a moment could I forget the time — or the 13.7 new species I had to average each day to reach 5,000 by the end of the year. The harder I ran, the more time sped up, like living each day in fast-forward. But even on a Big Year, I had to hit pause once in a while.

"Hey, Noah, let's walk down to the hummingbird baths," Johan suggested, "before Lisa takes us to see the Sunbittern."

"Hummingbird baths? Sure," I said.

"It's just a short trail," he said. "We might find a few other birds on the way. Roy, are you coming?"

"I think I'll stay and wait for you guys," Roy said. "Go ahead — I'll be here when you get back."

Johan smiled, stood up, grabbed his binoculars, and led the way into the forest. I ate the last bite of pancake and followed along, curious what we might see. Past the moth trap, which was now picked clean, the trail switchbacked through dense forest before dropping into a steep, wet ravine.

"Sometimes hummingbirds like to bathe in the stream below us," Johan said, "but this is a good area, close to the lodge, to see many different species."

He walked slowly, listening for rustling sounds and vocalizations while we descended a steep section.

We stopped to watch an Orange-billed Sparrow, a surprisingly cryptic bird for its striking appearance: black head with a white eyebrow and throat, olive green back, bright yellow shoulders, gray underparts, and the namesake neon-orange beak. It scratched quietly in the leaf litter, so unobtrusive that, had it sat still, I never would have seen it.

"Hey, Johan, why does Roy often seem like he has trouble breathing?" I asked.

"You noticed that he's very thin, too, right?" Johan asked. "Roy has had a difficult time in the past few years."

We watched the sparrow catch some type of small insect.

"Almost ten years ago," Johan continued, "in 2005, Roy was diagnosed with cancer — a type of leukemia. He fought it, but it left him with about fifty percent of his natural lung capacity. That's why he moves slowly now, and why he stayed back instead of walking on this steep trail."

"That means he was, what, in his mid-twenties?" I asked.

"Yes," Johan said. "It's hard to believe, isn't it? Obviously, it changed things. When he was diagnosed, he was almost completely sedentary for about two years. That's when Roy started painting a lot. Now he can be a guide, too, as long as he takes it steady."

I wondered whether this might have kindled Roy's all-encompassing interest in the natural world, and his fascination with the interconnectedness of various plants and animals of the forest. Many birders focus mostly on identifying species, but Roy took a grander view. His artwork depicted not only birds but also frogs, fish, ants, butterflies, snakes, caimans, sloths, monkeys, jaguars, flowers, trees, and landscapes. He painted people, too: kayaking, surfing, dancing, and playing musical instruments. His natural subjects were realistic, but Roy painted people in a looser, freer style, with bright colors flung across the canvas in energetic drips

and spatters. All of the images were colorful and uplifting, captur-
ing Costa Rican life in its full, vibrant *pura vida*.

The trail ended at a set of benches overlooking a shady stream,
which had several shallow pools.

"These are the hummingbird baths," Johan said. "The hummers usually come here in the afternoon, maybe to rinse off that
sticky sugar water."

We sat for a minute while nothing stirred. Then, like a tiny
mirage, a Crowned Woodnymph appeared over one of the pools,
hovering inches above the water. It was violet-blue and green, iridescent on its entire three-inch body. After a little hesitation, it
dipped into the water once, twice, then zipped away again, having
bathed entirely in midair.

The whole bath took just a few seconds. There was something
magical about it, as if catching a fairy in an unguarded moment. I
wondered how few people on Earth have ever watched a hummingbird bathe — a rare treat. We retraced our steps to the lodge. Lisa
appeared and checked her watch.

"Just give me a minute," she offered, "and I can take you to look
for a couple of staked-out birds nearby — including that Sunbittern. We'll be quick, because I know you guys need to keep moving."

While Lisa ran off to grab her keys, I pulled out my phone to
check email on the lodge's Wi-Fi network and found a message from
John Cahill, a young birder in Guatemala. I'd never met John but
knew who he was. His family had moved to Guatemala when he was
five years old, and he'd grown up learning the birds of his adopted
country. Now nineteen, John was so obsessed with birds that he had
dropped out of high school to do his own Guatemala Big Year in
2014, recording an impressive 651 species while spending all but
twenty days of the year in the field.

"How is the Big Year?" he wrote. "Are you planning to be in

Guatemala? I'd love to show you some of the regional endemics and get you a step closer to 5,000!"

Reading John's email gave me goosebumps. Less than a day had passed since I'd learned of Hugo's death in a car accident, and soon I'd be arriving in Guatemala with no one to meet me. John had no idea that I had been planning to go birding with Hugo there. It really felt like Hugo's spirit had reached out and guided John to me. I silently thanked Hugo for sending this gift: now I had a new plan for Guatemala and a new friend to meet.

In the good company of Roy and Johan, I spent several more days exploring Costa Rica's rich birdlife. When it was time to say *adiós*, I had seen 413 species in the country — 158 new for the year — and averaged an incredible 22.5 new birds per day. My year list stood a little over 2,265 species, and I had reached an interesting milestone: I had found half of the birds in the entire Western Hemisphere before even setting foot in North America.

Costa Rica was followed by five whirlwind days with John in Guatemala — mostly in the highlands, where we saw more Resplendent Quetzals and actually got erupted on by a volcano. The Big Year rolled on, as life does, while millions of birds migrated north, as they do every year, flying free to chase the spring.

A couple of months later, in June, while I was tearing through Europe, Roy sent me a short message. He was in high spirits after taking a trip with friends into the Darién Gap in eastern Panama to look for nesting Harpy Eagles. Not only had the group seen the Harpy, but they had also observed nesting Crested Eagles — an even rarer raptor that I had missed. Roy was so happy that his report brought tears to my eyes.

A year after that, I heard that Roy celebrated the birth of his second daughter, then was diagnosed with cancer again, this time in the mouth. He underwent an eight-hour operation to remove most of his jaw, but didn't pull through. I learned of his passing from Lisa Erb.

"We are all very sad here in Costa Rica to have lost such a great naturalist, guide, artist, and friend," Lisa said. "His wife told me that his trip with you was a very special moment for him."

Lisa sent me a photo of the three of us — Roy, Johan, and I — smiling on the terrace at Rancho Naturalista. In the picture, Roy is wearing a T-shirt that says, "Caution: This person may talk about birds at any moment." When I looked at the photo, memories of my days with Roy in Costa Rica came flooding back.

Life's tragedies often come with blessings. With death, there is also life. The same month that I heard about Roy's death, Johan emailed me with the exuberant news that he was to have a second child, a son.

"Regards, my good friend," he said. "Just want to share with you that my wife Lauren is pregnant — it will be a baby boy and we are going to call him Noah! Noah Felipe Fernández Roman."

"Congratulations!" I replied. "How did you decide on the name?"

"We like your name," he explained, simply. "When someone asks him about it, Noah will have a great story to tell."

9

Home

AFTER AN EXHILARATING five-month run in South and Central America, I began to admit to myself the possibility not only of reaching the goal of 5,000 birds by the end of the year, but of substantially exceeding it. Barely a third of the way through the year, at the beginning of May, I was averaging 19.5 species a day — well above the 13.7 average needed to hit 5,000. If I could keep up this pace — and oh, how I hoped I could — the final tally might be a lot higher than anyone, including me, had guessed it could be.

But I tried not to think too hard about numbers as I left Central America and continued my northward migration to Mexico. To play the long game, I had to focus on small increments. And now I was entering the difficult "long middle" of this project — too far from either the start or the end to contemplate more than one step at a time.

I had a satisfying two weeks chasing the specialty birds of Mexico, divided between the southern state of Oaxaca and a lengthy transect across the north end of the country. In Oaxaca I met up with Eric

Antonio Martínez, an astute local birder who once led bird walks for tourists from cruise ships. He introduced me to eye-popping endemic birds as well as their gastric equivalent — the mouth-watering endemic black *mole* (pronounced "MO-lay") that is the signature dish of Oaxaca, rich in chocolate, sesame, peppers, and spices. One afternoon, atop the majestic ruins of Monte Albán, the ancient Mesoamerican city that stands on a flattened hilltop above Oaxaca, Eric and I watched a Slaty Vireo while the calls of Rock Wrens echoed from the pyramids. I wondered whether these birds had sung during the human sacrifices that occurred here 2,000 years ago.

Afterward, on the Pacific Coast in Mazatlán, a birder friend of Eric's named René Valdés hatched a bold but unexpected plan for us: we would drive straight across northern Mexico rather than hang around a resort town where bikinis outnumbered birds. That way, I could fly to the United States from Monterrey and have the chance for a few northeast Mexican species on the way. A few years ago such a road trip would have required crossing nearly impenetrable terrain, but René explained that an extraordinary new highway had just been pushed through the mountains, and he was chafing to explore its birding potential.

Until recently, traveling between the cities of Mazatlán and Durango meant braving the "Devil's Backbone" — an accident-prone, tortuous road across the rugged Sierra Madre mountain range. The landscape is so rough that when the road was constructed in the 1940s, mules were needed to carry supplies for the workers. Deep in the barrancas — steep gullies isolated by sheer topography and thick forests — lawlessness and wilderness have generally prevailed; for the past decade, the region has been largely controlled by drug cartels of the Sinaloa and Durango states, and traveling through the area was traditionally slow and dangerous.

But with the completion of the $2.2 billion superhighway in

late 2013, the Devil's Backbone was dramatically tamed. What had been a heinous eight-hour journey now takes just two and a half hours, much of the trip spent zipping through sixty-two tunnels and across 135 bridges. It is among the most amazing engineering feats of a country that knows a thing or two about engineering, all the way back to the pyramid-building age. The new four-lane free-way maintains an even 5 percent grade through unimaginably wild canyonlands, mostly by brute force; in one forty-five-mile section, a full eleven miles are tunneled through solid rock. At its crux is the cable-spanned Baluarte Bridge, which connects the states of Sinaloa and Durango and, at a vertigo-inducing 1,300 feet above the ground, is now the highest bridge in the Western Hemisphere — tall enough to fit the Empire State Building underneath with room to spare. It took more than a thousand workers several years just to build the bridge, in an area so remote that the first surveyors had to ride four hours by horseback to reach the site.

René and I set out from Mazatlán on May 16, and we rolled into the Sierra Madre with no traffic, no delays, and not a pot-hole in sight. The surface was smooth as glass, a welcome change from months of bumping around the teeth-jarring roads of rural South America. As we entered the mountains, the road seemed to lift off; its surface rarely stayed at ground level, and I had the feeling of swooping and diving around each obstacle like a bird in flight.

René told me that, soon after this highway was opened, most of the copper wiring was stolen from its tunnels, so security guards had to be posted at strategic spots. The road was also patrolled by federal police, who had rarely ventured up here before and who hoped to use the new access to combat illegal drug activities. For years these mountains were an unregulated haven for marijuana and opium poppy farms; Durango had become a flashpoint of conflict between the rival Sinaloa Cartel and Los Zetas gang, and

Durango City was briefly named one of the ten most dangerous cities in the world for its grisly murder rate. Besides speeding up commute times, the national government believed that this highway would bring modern development and the long arm of the law to an unruly region.

We stopped at several places to look for birds, not knowing exactly what we might find.

"This is all new territory for birders," René said. "We're still exploring what might be out here."

At the Baluarte Bridge, we parked and hiked down a gravel spur and watched a pair of Military Macaws fly gracefully through the canyon, their long green bodies mere specks beneath the bridge's lofty span. A Zone-tailed Hawk soared in a nearby thermal zone, and a Happy Wren sang happily from a thicket.

Down the road, at another side track, René and I stopped again to explore the scrubby forest on foot. A few minutes in, we rounded a corner and abruptly came face to face with two men armed with rifles. The men asked why we were walking there. René talked with them briefly and they continued on their way. Afterward, René told me that guns are technically illegal in Mexico except for hunting rifles, and that these guys were probably farmers out looking for game. A few minutes later we started hearing shots, seemingly at random, from several different directions; one went off uncomfortably close, right under a nearby tree. What the heck? We couldn't see anyone and I started to get nervous, but then realization dawned: the tree was covered with a vine that bore some type of air-filled fruit, and the fruits were exploding in the midday heat. Every time one popped, it gave off a sharp sound like a gunshot.

We arrived in Durango City — still a dusty cowboy town in the style of John Wayne and Clark Gable — by late afternoon, in time for a little birding in the surrounding hills. René wanted to find a Striped Sparrow, a Mexican endemic, and we had good looks at several before dusk, along with some old North American friends such as Acorn Woodpeckers, Western Bluebirds, and an Eastern Meadowlark. As darkness fell, we patrolled a dirt road among the pine trees, hoping to find a couple of nocturnal birds before calling it a day.

The Striped Sparrow put my year list at exactly 2,499 species — one short of the halfway mark. This was the best possible news, for it meant that my strategy for the year was working even better than I had planned. I originally expected that I would reach this milestone before leaving the Americas, and I hadn't yet touched United States soil. With a couple hundred more new species waiting for me in the States, I was feeling optimistic when, with my high-powered LED flashlight aimed into the dark Mexican forest, I spotted a speck of red eyeshine on the ground.

Spotlighting for animals at night, you're looking for their luminous eyes. Eyeshine is technically an effect of the *tapetum lucidum*, a layer of tissue behind the retina of some vertebrate animals that reflects light, allowing the eye's photoreceptors a second chance to process incoming signals. This gives nocturnal species their superior low-light vision, and the tissue is highly visible: if you direct light at an animal with a *tapetum lucidum*, its eyes will seem to glow in the dark. The color varies by species, and you can often guess the type of animal by its eyeshine. Cat and dog eyes glow iridescent green; horses and cows are blue; fish are white; and coyotes, rodents, and birds are red. (Primates, including humans, don't have a *tapetum lucidum*, so you won't see any eyeshine by spotlighting a person. The redeye effect in powerful flash photos is a reflection of blood vessels at the back of the eyeball.)

"René, do you see it?" I asked.

Instinctively, he leaned over my shoulder. To see eyeshine, you have to line up your own eyes with the light source.

"Yes, it's probably some type of nightjar," he said. "Let's see if we can get a little closer."

The two of us snuck toward the red glow, which was at ground level in an open area of the forest. As we approached, I began to make out the outline of a bird sitting on bare dirt. It had the typical shape of a nightjar, as René had predicted: horizontal, angular, with a chunky head at one end and a short tail at the other.

Nightjars, in the family Caprimulgidae, are a unique group of birds represented by about a hundred species on six continents. All of them are nocturnal, eat insects, are cryptically patterned, lay their eggs on the ground, and can be frustratingly tough to encounter. Some people call nightjars "goatsuckers," for the old folk tale that these birds steal the milk from goats at night (yet another bird myth promoted by Aristotle and later reinforced by Pliny). Several types are possible in northern Mexico, so we'd need a good look at this one to distinguish its field marks. Would we be able to get close enough?

René and I dropped to our knees and crept toward the nightjar, which sat unmoving on the ground. I kept the flashlight beam aimed at it, trying to discern the patterning of its plumage. It had a stocky shape with a hint of white in the throat, blackish cheeks, and buff-barred wing feathers, but mostly it just looked brown, like pretty much all nightjars do.

I snapped a fuzzy photo, crawled closer, snapped another photo, and wormed toward the bird until it was just a few feet away. Still, René and I couldn't decide if it was a Buff-collared Nightjar or a similar-looking Common Poorwill. I pulled out my phone, opened an app with the Mexican field guide, and compared the two illustrations side by side with the bird sitting in front of us. It didn't seem to mind.

"It looks all brown," I said. "I don't see any orange color on the nape."

"Ye-e-es," said René, sounding uncertain. "A Buff-collared Nightjar should have some color around its neck. But I dunno, it might be hidden by the feathers."

I inched forward until, to my surprise, only about a foot remained between my nose and the bird's bill. It still made no move to fly, apparently hypnotized by the beam of the flashlight. I'd heard that nightjars could sometimes be lulled in this way, but had never tried it before. Slowly, I reached out my left hand and, holding my breath, lightly stroked the feathers on top of the bird's head while it sat absolutely still, unblinking and unflinching.

My photos might show enough for a positive identification, I thought, but there was one way to be absolutely sure. Gently, I closed the fingers of my hand around the bird's body, using a technique I'd learned handling hundreds of bird species as a researcher for projects in various countries. The bird's head poked between my index and middle finger while its body rested comfortably in the palm of my hand, protected from sudden movements or injury. It didn't struggle when I picked it up, and it felt like palming a fluffy tennis ball off the ground.

René leaned in to inspect every feature. With my free right hand, I carefully extended one wing, spread out the tail feathers, and examined the underparts while the bird stayed frozen. Its eyes were open, and I could feel its heartbeat with my fingers, the only confirmation that it was alive.

"It's definitely a Common Poorwill," René concluded. "The patterns on the neck, wing, and tail are distinctive."

I looked up at him and smiled.

"That's it, then!" I said. "The 2,500th bird!"

To hold this halfway mark in my hand, as a living, breathing creature, underscored how little its number conveyed the thrilling, real-life experience. For a few more seconds I examined it, enjoying the rare privilege of such a close encounter with a fascinating species. The Common Poorwill is the only bird in the world known to enter torpor for extended periods; in some places, poorwills have been shown to maintain a catatonic state, like hibernation, for several months during winter. Maybe that explained this bird's extraordinary calmness.

To set it free, I uncurled my fingers so that the poorwill balanced on my flattened palm. When I switched off the flashlight, I could feel it there, letting its eyes readjust to darkness. After a minute, the bird seemed to awaken from its trance; its little feet scratched against my skin, and then, with a soft flutter, it spread its wings, took flight, and disappeared quietly into the Durango night.

+ - + - +

Two days later, on May 18, I landed in Houston, Texas, with shaggy hair, a farmer tan, and a thick coating of Mexican dust on my clothes. It was strange to think that my Latin American leg was already over. I handed my passport to the immigration officer and watched him flip through the stamped pages: Antarctica, the Falklands, Argentina, Chile, Brazil, Peru, Ecuador, Colombia, Panama, Jamaica, Costa Rica, Guatemala, Mexico.

"Doing a bit of traveling, huh?" he asked. "What have you been up to in all these places?"

"Birdwatching," I said, hoping he'd just let me through.

"Huh," he said, not looking up.

I'd lately discovered that a disheveled, single male traveler with a backpack and a passport full of stamps tends to raise eyebrows at immigration points, and I'd honed my story. Oddly, the sillier it sounded, the more people seemed to believe it, and so, instead of vague explanations like "I'm a tourist" or "traveling to see friends," I just told the truth. When asked, I offered that I was trying to set a world record of birdwatching. Most border officers couldn't think of any follow-up questions. Who would make up such a ridiculous cover story?

I had learned my lesson the hard way in Jamaica, the only place during the year where immigration really detained me. On the entry form, I put "writer" as my occupation. When the officer read the form, he jumped right in with questions.

"What kind of writer are you?" he asked.

"I write books," I said.

"Well, what kind of books?" he pressed.

"Books about birds," I said.

"What birds? Can I see one of your books?"

"All kinds. I write about all kinds of birds. Sorry, I don't have any books with me."

"Hmm. What are you doing in Jamaica, then?"

"Looking for Jamaican birds."

The man became increasingly suspicious, asking a litany of questions. He read every line of my form, and eventually jabbed at a line near the bottom with his index finger.

"You haven't listed a local address," he said.

"That's because a friend is picking me up and I don't know where we're staying," I said.

"You must have a local address. You can't pass. Step back, sir, please. Next!"

Brusquely kicked out of the immigration line, feeling embarrassed and denied entry into Jamaica on my first attempt, I wandered around in limbo while everyone else from my flight was checked through to customs. Eventually, I found a wall advertisement for a luxury hotel and copied its address onto my form. Then I scribbled out "writer" and, in its place, wrote "BIRD MAN" as my new occupation.

When I approached the counter again, it was the same man, but he acted like he hadn't seen me just half an hour ago. Instead of asking questions, he smiled, scanned my form, stamped it, and filed it.

"Have a great visit!" he said, and I walked straight through.

So that was the trick. You just have to fill in every blank, and the wilder your responses the better. After that lesson in Jamaica, I wrote down random hotel addresses on immigration forms — often ridiculously expensive, five-star establishments — and always called myself a "bird man." Nobody, anywhere, ever said a word.

The United States official in Houston was no different. Snapping shut my passport, he slid it briskly across the counter.

"Welcome home!"

✦ ✦ ✦

It was sweet to hear those words at a border crossing. For the next week and a half I'd be in my home country. I would even spend a couple of nights in my own bed before moving on for the rest of the year. As I walked past the baggage claim into a warm Texas afternoon, I could feel parts of me relaxing that hadn't unclenched in nearly five straight months in Latin America.

Somehow, down south, I could never let go of the feeling of being on guard. In the front of my mind, I was always aware of the logistics; in the back of my mind, I was always ready for something to go wrong. Because few of the places I visited were familiar, each day presented a series of little decisions that, at home, I don't even think about: Where is the nearest electrical outlet? Can you rinse your toothbrush in the sink? What's for breakfast? How do you adjust the showerhead without electrocuting yourself? Collectively, all of these small questions keep you engaged, but they are also taxing, and they prevent you from settling into a routine.

The farther I traveled, the more on edge I felt. I always knew how far away I was from home, both physically and figuratively, even if on an unconscious level. This is something innate to all of us: as humans, when we explore the far horizons, we need a base to return to. Nobody can be a true nomad forever, as alluring as that might sound; we all crave a place of our own.

I hadn't quite realized how much I'd missed home until I walked under an airport sign that said, "Welcome to the USA." That sign made me excessively happy — not from patriotism especially, but from a sense of letting go, knowing that, for the next stage, I'd be on well-known territory. I didn't even care that it was Texas, which might as well be a foreign nation to me. Outside the Houston airport, I looked at the big cars, the road signs in English, the steakhouses, the sprawling gas stations, and even the hitchhikers with the giddy feeling of coming home after a long sojourn in the wilderness. It was as exciting to visit my own country now as it had been, months ago, to leave it.

I had no time to slow down, though. This border crossing began a new phase — a sprint across the United States and Europe, with little space to rest. For the next three weeks I'd board a flight, on average, once every two and a half days during the short, intense northern summer.

When I set up my itinerary I'd intentionally planned a mad dash through North America and Europe. It simply wasn't worth more time. Ironically, the three continents with the most birders have, by far, the fewest birds: the United States, Europe, and Australia each host fewer than half as many species as South America, Asia, or Africa. Diversity concentrates in the tropics, so, strategically, I focused my efforts on the most species-rich areas. It's also easier to get around with First-World infrastructure, making it possible to blitz from one bird to the next in the United States and Europe, slashing the time needed for these destinations.

My United States leg would be short and sweet: after two days in Texas, I'd scheduled two days in southeast Arizona, two days in

Southern California, several days at home in Oregon, and one day in New York before flying to the Eastern Hemisphere for the rest of the year. It seemed laughably short, but numbers drove my itinerary. I was aiming for specific bird targets, and I would move lightly and quickly to get them.

At the Houston airport I was met by Michael Retter, a friend who had recently moved to Dallas and had volunteered enthusiastically for a two-day road trip in his adopted state. He was waiting when I arrived, and, as the afternoon light faded, we jumped in his car.

"We've just got time," he said, "to see one good bird before it gets dark! Did you see a Worthen's Sparrow this morning, by any chance?"

"Uh, yes, I did," I said, "outside of Monterrey."

"Good!" said Michael. "Because I doubt if anyone has ever seen a Worthen's Sparrow" — endemic to northeast Mexico — "and a Red-cockaded Woodpecker on the same day. That would be a neat trick!"

Michael explained that he'd reached Houston a little early, so he'd stopped to scout a patch of pinewoods near the airport while my plane was landing. There he'd found a Red-cockaded Woodpecker — an endangered species of the southeast United States — and, because this might be my only shot at seeing one this year, we were now headed back to see if we could locate it again.

While we drove toward the stakeout, Michael outlined his ideas for the rest of our route around Texas: First we'd hit the pinewoods for a few species like this woodpecker, then slide down the central Gulf Coast to pick up some key shorebirds. After that, we'd hightail it to the hill country of central Texas for two endemic nesters, the Black-capped Vireo and Golden-cheeked Warbler, before perhaps streaking down to the southern tip of the state for any remaining targets. It was a lot for two days, but the freeways around here had a posted speed limit of eighty-five miles per hour, and Michael was willing to drive all night if necessary.

"Excellent!" I said. "Let's go for it!"

Texas is a great birding state with well-established hotspots, and it was just a matter of connecting the dots to find each species. But my must-see list here was a little unusual, as Michael observed. The birds that people typically look for in Texas were mostly ones I'd already seen: either Mexican specialties that barely make it across the border (which I'd already found in Mexico) or long-distance migrants that accumulate along the coast during spring (which I'd already seen on their wintering grounds in Central America). On my shopping list were locally common birds that normally wouldn't seem very exciting: Blue Jays, Tufted Titmice, Carolina Wrens, and other backyard residents. I had already recorded the rarities elsewhere — in the places where they were common.

But the Red-cockaded Woodpecker, which isn't common anywhere, presented an exquisite exception. These woodpeckers are persnickety about where they live, digging cavities only in the trunks of live, mature, longleaf pine trees in scattered patches of savanna forest between Texas and the Carolinas. That pickiness hasn't helped their populations adapt to a shifting landscape, and today the Red-cockaded Woodpecker is listed as an endangered species. Their nesting areas are now heavily managed and monitored to protect the birds that remain.

Michael's woodpecker spot was a ten-minute drive from the international terminal, and we arrived just before sunset.

"These birds can be sort of lazy," he warned as we walked into the forest. "Each evening, they climb into their tree cavities to roost for the night. Sometimes they go to bed early. I hope we're not too late."

He pointed at a tree with a garish white stripe of paint around the base of its trunk.

"It's easy to find Red-cockaded Woodpecker nesting sites because many of them are marked," he said. "Researchers paint the trees to help monitor populations."

The two of us stood a hundred yards away and watched quietly. Luckily, our timing was perfect: right after sunset, a bird swooped in, landed on the tree, and announced its presence with a loud *queeck* like the sharp sound of a squeeze toy.

The woodpecker was small, less than nine inches from bill to tail, and intricately patterned with black and white over its entire body. Its cheeks were bright white, helping distinguish this bird from other small black-and-white woodpeckers like the Downy and Hairy. It hitched vertically up the bark, moving in jerky spasms toward the entrance of its cavity. In the distance I could hear one or two others *queeck*-ing back and forth; the Red-cockaded Woodpecker is unusual for living in social groups, with multiple roosting sites on each territory, and I supposed they were bidding each other goodnight after another long day of pounding their heads on pine trees.

With one quick heave, the woodpecker dove into its hole. Its head appeared at the entrance for a few seconds, as if taking one last look before going to sleep, then retreated inside.

"That's it!" said Michael. "Come on, we have a ways to go tonight."

With a sigh, I turned to follow him out of the forest. The woodpecker was at home, but I was just passing through. Even in my own country, I seemed to be a visitor, never quite satisfied with where I stood at any given moment. As long as there were more birds to see, I had to keep flying on and on and on.

When I did finally reach home, I couldn't settle. In my original plans, I'd allowed several days at my house near Eugene, Oregon, as the only rest stop during the year. In late May, almost at the midpoint of my round-the-world journey, I thought it might be nice to hang around home for a little while.

I had a few jobs to do, anyway: get a haircut, get my teeth cleaned, pick up my duplicate passport with visas for Africa and Asia in it, buy a new cell phone, replace my watch battery, purchase new shoes, swap worn-out clothes for replacements, spray my gear with mosquito repellent, and scarf down my mom's fresh-baked chocolate chip cookies. Those tasks took half a day. But then, accustomed to birding every single second, I couldn't help feeling restless. After one night in my own bed, instead of taking it easy, I called up a couple of friends, Dan and Anne Heyerly, and asked if they'd like to go birding for a couple of days.

I'd known the Heyerlys since I was about twelve years old, attending meetings of the Southern Willamette Ornithological Club in Eugene. Dan, a retired real estate appraiser, and Anne, a pharmacist, met through the group and were married a few years later. When I was a teenager they often took me on local excursions, encouraging my interest, and they had done as much as anyone to help guide my passion for birds. Now they liked to vacation in far-flung destinations such as India and Morocco on hardcore birding trips, wearing matching field gear and keeping their lists together. As friends and fanatical birders, they were closely following my progress.

"What are you missing?" asked Dan, getting right to the point.

"And do you think you'll reach six thousand by the end of the year?" pressed Anne.

She had been running some calculations of her own and thought I had a good chance of hitting 6K.

I'd already drawn up a list of bird targets in Oregon, and

I thought I might add fifty species in my home state. For once, I could enjoy being the local expert. It was fun to plot out routes on familiar turf.

"I could use a few coastal birds like Greater Scaup and White-winged Scoter," I said, "and it would be nice to see a Tufted Puffin, since I won't find one anywhere else. As for the final tally, who knows? I guess six thousand is possible!"

The three of us decided to hit the central Oregon coast, where a longstanding puffin colony would give us an almost guaranteed sighting of the charismatic birds. From Eugene it was a two-hour trip to Newport, a small city on the rocky shores of the Pacific Ocean, where we'd start working our way north to the puffins.

As we drove, I told Dan and Anne about my most recent stops in Arizona and California, which had been productive but tiring. In Arizona, birder friends John Yerger and Scott Olmstead of Tucson joined forces to exhaust nearly every possible species in two days, even venturing into the famed California Gulch, a remote canyon on the United States–Mexico border, to nab a skulking Five-striped Sparrow. Dan and Anne nodded with appreciation — they'd been there, too. Then, in Los Angeles, I spent two crazy days birding with a colorful cast of characters: a NASA asteroid physicist named Lance Benner; an entrepreneurial nonprofit CEO named Dave Bell; and a twelve-year-old superbirder named Dessi Sieburth, who had just been named the American Birding Association's "Young Birder of the Year" in an annual competition that I had also won as a teenager. Despite our differences, we shared an all-consuming passion for birds, and we stayed up each evening talking about little else.

Increasingly, as the Big Year rolled on, it seemed I was gaining a little celebrity, among birders at least. Word about my project had filtered out, and now I was being recognized each time I arrived in a new place. People told me they were following the blog, and many asked about my recent adventures. It was fun to be feted, but sometimes tiring. After a full day in the field, I often stayed up late as the guest of honor, adding to my deficit of sleep.

Dan, Anne, and I spent an easygoing day on the Oregon coast, hitting some scenic spots typical of our beautiful state. These places were all rooted in me from a lifetime of attachment, and I noted all the familiar details of the lighthouses, rocky promontories, shallow bays, and miles of towering sea cliffs. Sunshine lit up the landscape, and hardly a breath of wind licked the water. Lush, green forest lined pristine sandy beaches, unspoiled by development, where seals and otters frolicked in the sparkling breakers.

It was one of those idyllic summer days that people visiting Oregon hope to experience. After months of traveling, I had worried that my sense of awe would get jaded, but now I marveled anew at the natural assets of my home state — which, in 2015, was named the most popular state in the United States to move to. Having witnessed the whole range of spectacular scenery lately, I was glad that, for sheer magnificence, the Oregon coast compared favorably with just about anywhere.

Near the peaceful seaside town of Pacific City, Dan, Anne, and I stopped to look for the puffins. We set up our spotting scopes on a beach and aimed at offshore Haystack Rock. Tufted Puffins, like awkward clowns with enormous orange beaks and yellow head plumes, nest in burrows and cracks in the rock, where they can be seen flying and perching during the summer. Each year, pairs return to raise their chicks in the same burrows they used the previous season.

As we stood there in the late afternoon sunshine, I thought back to some of the other places I'd stood so far — from Antarctica to the top of the Andes, the Amazon to the Mexican wilderness. It felt just as satisfying to be here, where I knew the birds like friends and where my friends were birders. When this year ended, I knew I'd be content to come home.

"I've got one!" shouted Anne, peering through her scope. "It's flying clockwise around the back of the rock."

Dan and I watched the right side of the stack, where, sure enough, a football-shaped black bird with a neon-orange beak rocketed into view. This Tufted Puffin, my 2,701st species of the year, flew on stiff, paddle-shaped wings, flapping so hard that it seemed it could barely stay aloft. Those wings become flippers underwater, and puffins are one of the most elegant swimmers in the bird world, but it was hard not to laugh at the bird's clumsiness in the air.

A man on the beach stopped, stared at us with a curious expression, and asked what we were looking at.

"A puffin!" I said, keeping my eye glued to the scope.

"Oh, that's cool," he said, casting his gaze offshore. "I see them out on the water sometimes, when I'm on my surfboard."

He paused, surveyed the scene, and murmured, mostly to himself, "This place is incredible, isn't it?"

Just then, behind the puffin in my field of view, I saw a spout of water rise above the horizon — a whale taking a breath against the gathering sunset. In these calm conditions, it was easy to spot the blow from a great distance, and I watched the whale surface a couple of times in quick succession.

"Yes," I agreed, with a huge grin. "There's no place like home."

10

Missed Connections

I SHOULD HAVE KNOWN that my worst flight nightmare would come true in the United States. After months of smooth sailing with any number of dubious-looking airlines in Latin America, the wheels finally came off in New York. There, courtesy of United Airlines, I experienced the real-life embodiment of the nine circles of travel hell.

I couldn't seem to get out of the state. My first flight from Ithaca was delayed, then canceled, because the crew failed to show up. Rather than rebook me onto a flight with a later departure, the ticket agent stuffed me into a taxi bound for a completely different airport, where I waited out the rest of the afternoon, only to learn that a second flight was delayed, then canceled, because of thunderstorms. After that, in exasperation, I caught a Greyhound bus to New York City, arrived in the pelting rain at 2 a.m., crashed for a couple of hours at a Manhattan hotel, and managed to fly out the next day. By then I had been delayed for twenty-seven hours. It was a short, infinitely short, period of time in the space of a whole life, but an excruciating epoch within the confines of the Big Year.

None of this seemed to bother United in the least. Didn't they realize that time was of the essence? I had become a slave to time, and my blood was boiling. The airline that boasts the most flights to the most destinations around the world had offered me no flights to any destination, and in so doing had landed me with my second zero day of the year. Wasting time in airports wasn't quite what I'd envisioned for my last stop in the Western Hemisphere.

At least the previous day had gone well. After leaving home in Oregon, not to return until this year was over, I'd landed in Ithaca to meet Tim Lenz, a full-time programmer for the Cornell Lab of Ornithology's website, eBird, which I was using to track my sightings for the year. Tim spends his free time birding his brains out and knew where to find the species I sought in New York, partly because he'd catalogued them all in eBird. He was wiry, precise, and about the same age as me.

The two of us were near Cayuga Lake, looking for common birds such as Upland Sandpipers and American Black Ducks, when Tim received a WhatsApp message on his phone.

"Wow," he said, suddenly at full attention. "It looks like someone just reported a Brown Pelican flying over the lake. That's, like, the first inland record for New York! We've got to go see that bird!"

"Nice!" I said, and then I paused. "But, Tim, I just saw thousands of Brown Pelicans on the Pacific Ocean last week, where they're supposed to be. I don't need one for the year list. I do need to see American Black Ducks today because it's my last chance . . ."

Tim looked stricken. In this situation, it wasn't immediately clear which should take priority: a mega-rare species in New York for his life list or an ultra-common addition for my Big Year list.

"But it's a Brown Pelican!" he protested. "Do you realize how unusual that is? This might never happen again!"

I sympathized. In Oregon, whenever a rarity is reported, I leap to see it without a second thought. That's the nature of birding. You have to go for it because you don't know if it'll ever happen again. Still, for me, for the Big Year, this pelican sighting was a distraction.

"Maybe we can do both?" I suggested. "Do we have time to race over for the pelican, then go find some black ducks?"

"Yes!" Tim said. "Let's go for it!"

He pulled a big U-turn on the highway and, in moments, we were speeding toward Cayuga Lake on our new mission.

As we drove, Tim's phone blew up with WhatsApp messages from other birders on the pelican trail. Because Ithaca hosts Cornell University, with its famous Lab of Ornithology, the city is packed with birders — and all of them were now looking for the same Brown Pelican. Sightings were reported in real time via instant messages. Someone saw it flying south along the lake; someone else reported it a few miles away. The bird, for its part, apparently was roaming aimlessly around the forty-mile-long lake, probably wondering where it had taken a wrong turn from the ocean, unaware that its cover was blown.

A message pinged from Marshall Iliff and Tom Schulenberg, two of Cornell's elite birders, who suggested we head for a yacht club along the lakeshore. They were stationed up the lake and had just watched the pelican fly over their heads.

"It should pass by there in a couple of minutes if it continues straight," they said.

Tim got us to the marina in a hurry, and we ran onto the docks, scanning the skies. No pelican. How fast can a Brown Pelican fly? We stood there, trying to make hypothetical calculations of speed and distance, when Tim saw a speck on the horizon.

The long bill, dumpy body, and prehistoric-looking wings — even in distant silhouette — confirmed that we had our quarry. As the pelican approached, we raised our cameras like anti-aircraft gunners. The bird lumbered directly overhead, bomber style, giving full-frame views.

Tim was ecstatic.

"No way!" he said. "A Brown Pelican on Cayuga Lake!"

In another minute, it had disappeared in the direction of downtown Ithaca, where the WhatsApp reports kept coming. Someone reported it over the farmers' market, then a student on the Cornell University campus ran out of class and managed to see the bird fly over.

"That's quite a tick for the campus list," said Tim, with a connoisseur's appreciation.

We eventually found the American Black Ducks, for my benefit, but I couldn't stop thinking about that pelican and what it represented. On any scale smaller than the world, a Big Year is all about chasing rarities: if, say, you decided to limit your Big Year to New York State, then this Brown Pelican, or any other rarity, would be a must-see. Drawing the boundaries at the state line automatically puts you in reaction mode, with the imperative to tear off in any direction to witness one lost bird at a time. I have nothing against this sort of birding — I do it all the time — but some critics liken such pursuits to ambulance chasing, and at best it is a game of diminishing returns. Once you've seen all the common birds in a given area, it takes a lot more work and expense to find new ones.

The best way to avoid chasing rare birds is to take on the whole planet. You can go where each bird is supposed to be instead of waiting for a lost vagrant to show up on your doorstep. The world is the only scale that doesn't reward rarity hunts. I liked the idea that, by thinking globally and birding locally, I was helping to reinvent the Big Year as a way to appreciate the most common birds in their proper habitats. It seemed almost subversive, akin to a graffiti artist who paints murals instead of spraying his initials everywhere.

Well, it would be, I thought, if I could ever escape from New York. The global approach didn't work so well if you couldn't get out there.

Waiting for my flight, I'd watched the clock in despair as my next planned layover, in Iceland, shrank. By the time I finally saw New York City receding through my airplane window, the prospects in Iceland didn't look good: instead of a much-anticipated day and a half there, I'd now have only a few brief hours, and those hours would fall, naturally, in the middle of the night. With my new connection, I was scheduled to land in Reykjavik at midnight and take off again at 7 a.m.

My heart sank when I first saw the flight times. I figured Iceland was a write-off. But then I remembered something: at the height of summer, the sun stays up in the far north. It was June now, almost the longest day of the year. In Iceland it wouldn't get dark at all, which meant that, theoretically, I could still do some birding there on my short layover.

I contacted Yann Kolbeinsson, whom I had planned to meet in Reykjavik.

"Here's the deal," I said. "I'm supposed to land at midnight. I know that's a crazy time to go birding, but are you up for pulling an all-nighter? Otherwise I'll try to find a taxi and drive around for a couple of hours."

Yann quickly replied.

"Don't worry!" he said. "I'll pick you up when you get here, and we'll find as many birds as we can."

And that's just what happened. I arrived in Reykjavik a few hours later and found Yann standing in the moody, low-angled light of the midnight sun. He was a little taller than me, with brown hair and friendly features. In his pickup, we headed into the tundra surrounding the airport, just outside the city, to see what birds were around.

When I thanked him for meeting me so late, he brushed it off. Only later did I learn that Yann had driven five hours from his house in northern Iceland to meet me in Reykjavik, and then, after birding with me through the night, took a nap in his truck in the airport parking lot, drove five hours back home, and went straight to work the following day.

"It was worth it," he said, "to help with your Big Year! I wouldn't miss it!"

The land was treeless, volcanic, almost devoid of life, but Yann knew where to find the birds. We stopped at several points along the rocky coastline, where Iceland Gulls and Arctic Terns hovered over rafts of Common Eiders. Then, at about 3 a.m., we walked to a cliff with a colony of seabirds, including a Thick-billed Murre and, by great good luck, one Atlantic Puffin — a counterpart to the Tufted Puffin I'd seen in Oregon, and an iconic symbol of Iceland. The puffin crouched on a ledge outside its nesting crevice, its brightly colored bill sticking out like a navigational beacon.

I wondered how these Arctic birds get any sleep in the constant light of summer. They seemed to stay awake at all hours, catching naps whenever they felt tired. A few of the seabirds were snoozing where they perched on the rocks, but many others were energetically flying around, in defiance of the clock. I could relate. It had been days since I'd had a good night's sleep in a bed.

As my watch ticked toward 5 a.m., Yann and I scoped a large, marshy area on the outskirts of Reykjavik where Eurasian Wigeon, Whooper Swans, and other waterfowl gathered in large numbers. It was the most bird-filled spot we visited, and the greenest. Behind the wetland, an impressively large white building with a red roof stood alone on the flats.

"That's the presidential palace," Yann said.

"Wow," I said. "Imagine the yard list!"

The sun was rising again behind a veil of clouds, and its dusky light brightened into a new day. At sixty-four degrees of latitude, just a couple of degrees from the Arctic Circle, I had reached my farthest north for the year. It seemed fitting to celebrate this mark by staying up all night.

From here, things could only go south. I still had a long way to go, people to meet, and birds to see. This brief interlude in Iceland would later seem like a strange dream, sandwiched between North America and Europe, but for the moment my spirits were soaring.

By the time Yann dropped me off again at the airport, just before my connection to Norway, he had shown me thirty-six new bird species in less than seven hours. All of them were common in Iceland but rare elsewhere, which proved the point all over: you can wait forever for birds to come to you, but it's more sporting — and more logical — to go where they are.

The delay hadn't been too costly, thanks to Yann's help. We might have seen a few more species given an extra day, but in just a few hours we'd cleaned up practically every bird I'd hoped to find. After the Iceland all-nighter, on the 160th day of the year, my list stood at a respectable 2,786. I boarded my flight on Icelandair, where the mood lighting evoked the aurora borealis, the executive seats were called "Saga Class," and the attendants were all blonde, and sank deeply and gratefully into my seat. As the barren lands of Iceland slipped under the wings, I closed my eyes, imagined the president in his palace surrounded by ducks, and let sleep carry me softly into the eastern sky.

My only other significant airline snarl of the year came between Spain and West Africa, after a quick tour of the birds of Europe. In Norway, I joined a friend, Bjørn Olav Tveit, author of *A Bird-watcher's Guide to Norway*, whom I'd randomly met a few years earlier at a birding spot in Oregon, where he happened to be vacationing.

In Turkey, in the shadow of gigantic Easter Island–type statues near the top of Mount Nemrut, I chalked up the 3,000th bird of the year, a Tawny Pipit, with an enthusiastic young birder named Emin Yoğurtçuoğlu. And in Spain, Gorka Gorospe generously introduced me to some of the country's wealth of birds and presented me with a clever Big Year T-shirt he had designed himself. Nearly halfway through the Big Year, with the Americas and Europe under my belt and three-fifths of the way to my goal of 5,000 species, I still couldn't quite believe that my plans from a year ago were running like clockwork. Not a single local birder had left me stranded — in fact, birders around the world were embracing the spirit of this Big Year, going all out to contribute whatever they could.

But things went awry on the journey to Africa. When I checked in for what should have been an easy hop, I discovered that my flight to Ghana had flown the previous day. A day late and more than a thousand dollars short, I spent the rest of that afternoon haggling with agents before making a haphazard series of connections from Spain to Ghana by way of Germany and Ethiopia. It wasn't pretty, but it got me there.

As it turned out, the reroute wasn't a total loss. Faced with a painful five-hour layover in Frankfurt, Germany, during the daylight hours, I wondered if I might salvage some birds there instead of cooling my jets at the airport. When I opened Facebook on my laptop and typed "my friends in Frankfurt" in the search bar, a few names popped up, including one I recognized immediately: Peter Kaestner.

I'd long known about Peter but had never met or corresponded with him. Among world birders, Peter is legendary. For the past thirty-four years, he had worked for the U.S. State Department in more than a dozen countries, including Namibia, Colombia, Malaysia, Guatemala, Egypt, Papua New Guinea, Brazil, India, the Solomon Islands, and Afghanistan, specifically requesting postings in bird-rich destinations. As a strategy for observing a lot of birds in a lifetime, it's hard to beat, and by the mid-1980s Peter had seen a representative of every bird family in the world — the first person ever to do so. At one point he boasted the world's second-highest life list, and with more than 8,500 species, his is still ranked among the top ten. He even has a bird named in his honor: the Cundinamarca Antpitta, which I'd heard in April in Colombia, also known as *Grallaria kaestneri*.

I'd no idea that Peter was now posted in Germany, where he served as section chief at the U.S. Consulate General. It would be a thrill to meet him. I dispatched a short note before boarding my flight to Frankfurt, only half expecting a reply. A couple of hours later, when I touched down in Germany, I switched on my phone to find a text message: "We're waiting outside!"

Surprised and delighted, I ran out of the terminal and found Peter, who had come straight from work, dressed in a suit and running shoes. He had brought his wife, Kimberly, and they ushered me into their car.

"How long have we got?" Peter asked, as we pulled away from the curb.

"Just a couple hours," I said, and explained that, on this short layover, it would be difficult to find even one bird in suburban Frankfurt that I hadn't already seen.

"I think our only reasonable target here is the Gray-headed Woodpecker," I said, "which I missed everywhere else."

"Hmm," Peter said, and conferred with Kimberly. "Let's try a patch of forest near here, where we might run across a woodpecker."

We spent an hour rambling through a woodsy park, but there was little activity in midafternoon. The fresh air was welcome, though, and it was fun to talk to Peter and Kimberly, who had been following my progress.

"I'm glad to meet you," Peter said after a while, "because a world Big Year is something I've thought about but never taken seriously. But look, these woodpeckers are a slim chance. Isn't there anything else we can look for?"

"Well," I considered, "I suppose there is one other bird in Frankfurt, but it's hardly worth pursuing."

"Which one?" Peter asked quickly. "We might as well try."

"You're going to laugh," I said, "but I haven't seen an Egyptian Goose yet this year, and I think there is a feral population here. Right?"

Peter winced.

"Yes," he said, "Egyptian Geese are everywhere downtown. If that bird stands between you and a zero day, then we might as well go count one now."

With my time rapidly running out in Europe, the three of us drove to Frankfurt's historic center on a semiwild-goose chase. Technically, because Egyptian Geese have been established in Germany for years, I could count them, but they aren't native to Europe. Birders regard these introduced populations as trashy, and I would soon see plenty of wild Egyptian Geese in Africa. But it was still a tick — and one new bird today, mathematically speaking, would be infinitely better than zero.

It was absurdly easy to find the geese, which were loafing in an urban park on the Frankfurt riverfront when we pulled up.

"Ugly birds," Peter said, "but there you go!"

The three of us spent a few more minutes wandering downtown, admiring the more rarified sights of Frankfurt: the Frankfurt Cathedral, the famous Römer building, and a Monet exhibit. It was difficult to grasp that tomorrow I'd wake up south of the Sahara. These transitions between places and cultures always seemed strange, but they were getting to be strangely routine.

With a quick selfie in front of the cathedral, my United States–Europe leg wrapped up. Peter and Kimberly wished me well as we returned to the airport. I had one goose and two new friends to show for my serendipitous layover in Germany, and I was bound at last for Africa.

11

Kalu

PRACTICALLY NO ONE VISITS West Africa during the wet season, for good reason: the week before I arrived in Accra, the bustling capital of Ghana, severe flooding killed more than 150 people in the city. The coastal rainforest that grows like a sweat stain around the crook of Africa holds some of the world's greatest biodiversity and dozens of endemic bird species, and it generates a tremendous amount of rain. Because of my linear itinerary, I had no option but to visit during the monsoon. And so, on a dark and humid morning in late June, I pushed my way through the crowd in Accra, soaking in my first impressions of a wet and wild country.

From out of the horde of taxi drivers and hangers-on emerged a man who seemed to know me. He put out a hand and beamed.

"Noah, welcome to Ghana!"

"But how did you recognize me, Kalu?" I joked. In this throng, my blond hair stuck out like a neon sign.

"Come, let's go find our driver," he said, and led the way toward a busy parking area.

I'd contacted Kalu Afasi months ago after finding him through the BirdingPal website, but we'd exchanged only a few emails, so I was glad to see him now. He was thirty-eight years old, thin but athletic looking, with close-cropped hair and toned arms. He wore a T-shirt, loose khaki pants, and scuffed white tennis shoes.

"I waited for you here yesterday," he said. "I guess you were delayed?"

"Yeah, sorry about that," I replied. "I sent you a message, but maybe it was too late. My flight was canceled, so I spent yesterday in Germany, of all places."

"Don't worry! We are here now! It is all good! Here, let me introduce you to our driver, Yaw."

A smaller man appeared from a parked 4x4 and insisted on loading my backpack into the trunk, which was full of water jugs and other gear.

"He's called Yaw, which means 'born on a Thursday,'" Kalu said. "So if you forget, you can just call him 'Thursday.'"

I laughed, but Kalu seemed to be fascinated with birth days of the week. He asked which day I was born on, and I admitted I wasn't sure. Later, when we met a man who said he was born on a Saturday, Kalu looked chagrined.

"Bad luck," he said. "On Saturdays you must get up early to work on the farm because there is no school. That is not a good day to be born."

The three of us, under Yaw Boateng's steady hand, merged into Accra's congested traffic and navigated south under a dirty gray sky.

The road was jammed with tiny hatchbacks, beat-up passenger vans, and buses, many of them painted red and yellow. On both sides of the street, wooden stalls under umbrella canopies sold charcoal, cell phones, plantains, desk fans, toilets, sound systems, dresses, eggs, shoes, cement bricks, mattresses, electrical plugs, ice cream, bicycles, T-shirts, plastic containers, and anything else one might pop out for. Every so often we passed a dense market of fruit, vegetable, and meat stands doing a thriving open-air business. Many people balanced objects on top of their heads — pineapples, bowls, gas cans. Most were brightly dressed: schoolchildren wore crisp uniforms, women had flowing fabrics and flip-flops, and men sported spotless white shirts as if defying the red earth beneath their feet. Goats, dogs, and chickens dodged traffic, and extensive mud puddles attested to the recent rains. The air was thick with humidity, wood smoke, exhaust, and the heavy smells of sewage and cooking.

The country of Ghana, wedged between Côte d'Ivoire, Burkina Faso, and Togo, is a tall rectangle sitting on the horizontal part of Africa's western coast. Among its neighbors it is a small but relatively stable nation and has been popular for birders because of its accessibility and diversity. In a short trip, it's possible to reach the ocean, mountains, wet and dry forest, and even, in the northern part of the country, wide savannas and grasslands.

Kalu sat shotgun, twisting in his seat to talk above the engine noise.

"I was happy to receive your first email," he said, "because hardly anyone comes to Ghana this time of year. And I like your project. To travel the world and look at birds, what an amazing journey!"

"It's good to be in Africa," I said. "This is the only continent I have never visited before, so everything is new today."

"Especially the birds!" said Kalu.

"Yes," I agreed. "Almost all of the birds here will be lifers for me."

He looked pleased.

"We will see how many we can find in eight days," he said. "Basically, our plan is to start in the wet forests in the south — that's where we are heading now — then work our way north to the interior. I think maybe we can get three hundred species."

"Just hope it doesn't rain too much," I said.

"Don't worry about the weather!" Kalu replied. "We can't control it, and these days we can't even predict it. For the past few years, the wet season has been very strange; nobody knows when the rains will come. The climate is changing here."

I'd heard versions of this story in an unsettling number of places this year, and many of the birders who accompanied me had complained about unpredictable seasons. It was difficult to tease out other effects, like deforestation and overharvesting, but my view of global climate change had shifted lately after hearing enough local people talk about it. It wasn't just something for academics and politicians to argue about; these changes were already affecting those who depended on the land and environment.

We rode in silence for a while as Yaw piloted our 4x4 away from the city's congestion. Busy street scenes gradually gave way to open fields, skinny cows, palm trees, and kids on motorbikes.

I gazed out the window and thought about the coming months. After Ghana, I was scheduled to visit Cameroon, South Africa, Madagascar, Kenya, Tanzania, and Uganda before moving on to Asia. For me, all of these destinations were new, and Africa felt like the most exotic place I had yet traveled to. Its people, culture, landscape, and birds were so different from anything I'd ever experienced that I wasn't sure what to expect. The feeling of hyperawareness had returned after a relaxed stretch in the United States and Europe. For most of the rest of the year, I'd be passing through rural, tropical developing countries, and now I slipped back into the vigilant mindset I'd cultivated earlier in Latin America.

One of the benefits of returning to the tropics, I reflected, would be a more regular schedule. Each day near the equator includes a glorious twelve hours of darkness, which meant I could start catching up on the sleep that I'd sacrificed during the long days of northern summer. Also, because of Ghana's bumpy roads and diverse forests, the pace of travel would slow down. Kalu had arranged for us to stay in the same hotel, called the Hans Cottage Botel (yes, with a B), for the next two nights, and I appreciated the chance to sleep in the same bed twice for the first time in nearly a month — and maybe even rinse out my grimy, sweat-stained clothes.

For my first session of African birding, we stopped on an unmarked gravel road through scrubby fields, at a place called the Winneba Plains.

"Let's spend a couple of hours walking here," Kalu said. "Tomorrow we'll reach the forest, but this habitat has a few species we won't see anywhere else."

The two of us wandered down the track while Yaw stayed with our vehicle. Birds appeared everywhere, many with unfamiliar names: gonoleks, tchagras, and whydahs. A Guinea Turaco, dressed in green with black and white eye shadow, took flight with a startling flash of red wings, swooping across the path in front of us. I struggled to keep up, reveling in the feeling of being a little overwhelmed. Even the most common birds, such as Bronze Mannikins and Pied Crows, were fresh and exciting.

"Oh, look, look!" said Kalu, flinging his arm to gesture at a large bird lifting above the grass. "A Black-bellied Bustard!"

We watched the bustard fly with laborious wingbeats until it dropped behind a distant set of bushes. It looked distinctive, the size and approximate shape of a peacock, minus the tail, with white wings and a dark body, spindly neck and long legs.

"That is the bird I was most hoping to see here," Kalu explained. "Bustards are so good at hiding in the long grass, sometimes they are tough to find. Good thing it decided to fly just now!"

After two hours, we had recorded thirty-eight species, thirty-six of which I'd never seen before. As my introduction to Africa,

Ghana was giving me a crash course. It felt almost like being a beginner again.

$$+-+-+$$

That evening at dinner, I asked Kalu how he first became interested in birds. We ate at a restaurant with no walls. I faced a large bowl of fufu: a ball of pounded cassava dough floating in a soupy mixture of vegetables, spices, and chunks of gristly goat meat. Instead of utensils, I had been given a smaller bowl of tap water to cleanse my fingers.

"Just use your right hand," Kalu said. "Break off a piece of the dough and dip it in the broth. Delicious!"

I soon got the hang of eating soup one-handed, without a spoon — messy, but tasty.

Kalu took a bite, delicately rinsed his hand, and launched into a fascinating story.

"I am originally from Nigeria," he said, "where my father is a traditional king of sixteen villages. He is a very powerful man. I have a brother and sister, but I am the oldest, so I was supposed to become the next king there."

He paused.

"But I don't want to be a village ruler — too much drama! And can you imagine a king who watches birds all the time?"

Another pause.

"Anyway, when I was younger," Kalu said, "I wanted to do something else. So I started playing football, what you call soccer. Eventually I joined a Champions League in Nigeria, and then, sixteen years ago, moved to Ghana to play for a professional Champions League here. My dream was to join a national team — in fact, I was going through the process of becoming naturalized in Burkina Faso to play for their national football team, but that fell through. I never quite reached that level, but I did play professionally for a few years, and traveled all over Africa for matches."

Kalu was not particularly interested in birds until one day, sitting down in an Internet café here in Ghana, he signed up for a website that connects pen pals. The site matched him with a sixty-two-year-old birdwatcher from Denmark who had been making regular birding trips to Ghana since the 1990s. The two corresponded, and Kalu joined the Danish man on his next visit to Ghana.

That wonderful trip was an eye opener. Kalu's Danish friend taught him to examine field marks and identify each species, and he gave Kalu a book with illustrations of common African birds. Kalu, inspired, started going out on his own, and became so obsessed with birds that he missed physical therapy appointments and football practices, and got suspended from the team.

"When we were training on the beach, I'd be off looking for birds," he said. "That's how I got suspended."

Kalu decided to retire from football and become a birdwatching tour guide. He had too many injuries — a shoulder that often popped out of its socket, bad knees — and saw a new opportunity in birding. He saved his paychecks, bought a pair of binoculars, and then, when he figured he had enough, told the football team that he wanted to quit. It wasn't a smooth transition. Because he was still under contract, the football club took him to court to keep playing. And when his family realized what was happening, they organized a surprise "intervention" at Kalu's house to ask if he was going crazy.

"They couldn't believe I was looking at birds all the time," he said.

The next time the Danish man came to Ghana, Kalu joined him again, this time as a bird spotter. The Dane was so impressed that, when he returned home, he listed Kalu's name and contact information on BirdingPal — where I had discovered him — and Kalu started receiving requests to help other visitors. He was hired by an ecotour company for a while, learned the trade of guiding tourists, and eventually decided to go out on his own. He is now a full-time guide specializing in birdwatching tours, booked solid through the high season from October to May.

His family saw that it was good business and now they support Kalu's new profession.

"When did you last go back to Nigeria?" I asked, goat soup running down my forearm.

"It was two years ago, to help with a tricky situation," Kalu said. "Recently a lot of people in my village have converted to Christianity, including my father. Nearby, we have a patch of forest that has never been disturbed because, according to traditional beliefs, it is home to the gods. Nobody would dare hunt anything in that forest. But now people think that the devil lives there, and they want to burn down the forest to get rid of the devil. They also destroyed some nearby shrines that were more than a thousand years old."

Kalu looked serious.

"You don't have to believe in it anymore, but why destroy those things? Just leave them. They could be interesting for tourists! And the trees have nesting hornbills, which need large cavities. Burning them down would only hurt the wildlife."

We concentrated on our soup for a while, using the fufu like Indian naan bread to scoop up the meat and vegetables. In Africa, as I would soon discover, it is traditional in many places to eat with your hands, and the food is typically simple and delicious: plain starch, meat, and veggies.

"Well, it's great to hear that you can make a living from birding here," I said.

"Yes," Kalu said. "Of course, it hasn't been so easy this year because of the Ebola crisis. Five of my tours were canceled, almost my whole season — a year's work. I am calling this the 'Year of Ebola.'"

Several months had passed since the outbreak, which killed 12,000 people in West Africa in late 2014 and early 2015. Before my Big Year started, I thought I might run into Ebola in Africa. As it turned out, throughout the epidemic, the country of Ghana did not record a single case — the United States had more Ebola than Ghana did — but the scare crushed tourism across the entire region. People in countries as far away as Kenya and South Africa later told me that they had trips canceled, too, even though they were thousands of miles away.

"It's all Africa to the outside world," one person commented. "Like we're just one big, messy country."

Traces of the Ebola epidemic were still evident. The airport in Accra had a temperature scanner mounted in front of the immigration line, checking for fever among incoming passengers, but at this point it was a formality. Kalu told me that, during the height of the epidemic, he had been so "angry at Ebola" for wiping out his business that he signed up for Ghana's volunteer task force and attended emergency preparation trainings; if the disease had crossed Ghana's borders, he would have shuttled patients to the hospital and helped fight it on the ground. But that never happened, and the tour business dried up.

"A million people die of malaria every year, but nobody cares," he said. "Ebola was front-page news."

With that, he stood up.

"But enough of me talking. We will have an early morning," he said, "so we should both get some rest. Tomorrow, weather permitting, will be a fantastic day!"

+ + +

When most people picture Africa, they imagine the dry savannas of the east and south, but the rainforest in southern Ghana lies worlds away from those landscapes. Wet, brooding, and nearly impenetrable, the West African jungle is a tangled mess — more *Heart of Darkness* than *The Lion King*.

At Kakum National Park, it's hard to see the forest for the trees. The dense vegetation here reduces visibility so that you might be surrounded by exotic wildlife and never know it. Lush rainforests like this are a challenge: even though diversity is high, it's possible to walk for hours and not glimpse a single bird. Sunlight barely penetrates to the ground, and the trees are so tall that canopy-loving species stay hidden above a curtain of foliage. The calls of invisible birds seem to mock any attempt to lay eyes on them.

In 1995, to help visitors experience this jungle without a Kurtz-like breakdown, Ghana's Wildlife Division came up with a bright idea: working with the United States–based group Conservation International, they constructed a series of hanging walkways 130 feet off the ground at Kakum National Park, like a trail system in the sky. They built sturdy observation platforms around seven of the tallest treetops and linked the platforms with cable and rope bridges for a heightened perspective of the forest. The 1,100-foot-long walkway was opened on Earth Day, instantly transforming a once-obscure forest into a premier eco-attraction.

"It gives us a bird's-eye view," Kalu said, as we climbed into the canopy with a park guard before sunrise. "Now the birds have nowhere to hide!"

Mist rose gently while moisture dripped from millions of green leaves; thick clouds scudded and swirled, and I could feel humidity pressing down like a moist blanket. Just a day ago I had posed in front of the Frankfurt Cathedral with Peter Kaestner, but Europe already felt like a distant memory.

The morning chorus of birdsong was in full swing, and in the half-dawn, Kalu pointed out a few species by ear.

"Hear that constant *oop, oop, oop*? That's a Yellow-throated Tinkerbird in one of the treetops . . . And there's a Tambourine Dove calling down below us, the accelerating series of low-pitched *pu-pu-pu-pupupupu* notes . . . In the distance, a Klaas's Cuckoo — the sound quickly rises and falls."

I noted each of these auditory detections, though I hoped we would be able to get visuals, too. All of them were new for me.

As the sky brightened into day, birds began to appear. A pair of enormous shapes skimmed overhead and Kalu shouted, "Black-casqued Hornbills!" The hornbills, a bulked-up counterpart to the toucans I'd seen in South America, flew slowly over the treetops, showing off their protruding beaks and black bodies with white tail tips.

A subtle movement in a vine tangle caught my attention, and out popped a tiny bird with a streaky head and yellow belly: a Tit-hylia, Africa's smallest bird species (hummingbirds aren't found in the Eastern Hemisphere). I propped my binoculars on the railing of the observation platform to absorb eye-level views, more than a hundred feet high. Looking down past my feet, I couldn't even see the ground.

We passed slowly from one platform to the next, crossing a series of hanging spans. Each bridge had a single board, about eight inches wide, to walk on. Metal cables functioned as handrails, and ropes were knotted into a safety barrier about waist high. The length of each span varied, but most were about a hundred yards — enough to vibrate like a wobbly slackline — from tree to tree.

I had climbed several canopy towers in other places, including Ecuador and Costa Rica, but none could compare to this system of walkways. It continued on and on, tiptoeing and swinging across the forest, draped through the treetops like a string of Christmas lights. The bridges were unstable viewpoints, so Kalu and I, shadowed by the silent park guard, spent most of our time spotting birds from the platforms in between. When a flock moved through the canopy, we used the walkways to follow along.

Kalu pointed out a small shape hitching along a gnarly limb overhanging one of the bridges.

"That's a Melancholy Woodpecker," he said. "See how it's mostly green, streaked underneath, with a stubby tail?"

I snickered. "That's a funny name," I said, as I watched the woodpecker pick off a stray grub. "Almost as good as the Shining Sunbeam, or Wandering Tattler, or Oleaginous Hemispingus."

"There are some strange bird names in the world," Kalu agreed. "Just wait until you hear the Jackass Penguins in South Africa."

"Or the Diabolical Nightjar in Indonesia," I said. "That one sounds scary — its other name is Satanic Nightjar."

Kalu thought for a moment, then exclaimed, "Don't forget boobies and tits!"

"Yes, yes, all right," I laughed. "Let's keep our eyes on this pecker."

The Melancholy Woodpecker, for its part, didn't seem particularly downcast. With a sharp rattle call, it took wing and darted away through the canopy.

A squall swept through near midday, shutting down bird activity, and Kalu reluctantly announced it was time to go. In a few hours of hanging out, we'd recorded more than fifty species of birds from the Kakum walkways, almost all of which were new to me — a phenomenal experience. The three of us descended carefully to the mud at ground level, where Yaw was waiting with the 4x4 at park headquarters. Kalu and I thanked the guard and waved goodbye. We rolled out, heading north, while a steady rain soaked the forest.

✦ ✦ ✦

I'd agreed to cover our expenses in Ghana, but Kalu had an issue with his bank and couldn't accept wire transfers or PayPal.

"Don't worry," he said, "we can get cash from ATMs."

At home I'm the sort of person who swipes a credit card for every tiny purchase, but credit doesn't go far in the world's rural corners, so I had lately become accustomed to using cash everywhere. I carried multiple debit and credit cards and survived on ATMs. This strategy worked fine, but sometimes it got a little farcical.

In Colombia, for instance, I forgot to look up the exchange rate before visiting an ATM, where I needed to withdraw a few hundred dollars. Feeling lazy, I decided to make a rough calculation from the price of a Coke, which was posted at the next-door market. The soda was listed as two thousand pesos — wait, two *thousand*? If that was about fifty cents, then four hundred dollars would be . . . more than a million pesos! Hoping that I wasn't about to bankrupt my account, I punched in a 1 followed by six zeros. It worked out to $340.

I hadn't had a chance to hit an ATM in Ghana before Kalu whisked me into the forest, so after leaving Kakum National Park I reminded him of this errand.

"Yes," he said, "I know of one machine in Cape Coast, where we can stop this afternoon."

By the time we reached the city, Ghana's sixth-largest metropolis, rush hour had clogged the streets with every imaginable type of transport, from cargo trucks to mule carts. Motorbikes flowed around larger vehicles like sand in a sieve, and cows and goats wandered through traffic at about the same speed. Near the city center, thousands of people blanketed the sidewalks, spilling out of markets and open-air buildings.

In the midst of this activity, Kalu stopped us on a busy corner.

"Just around the block," he said, "is a Barclay's Bank with an ATM on the sidewalk."

"Great!" I said, and jumped out of the 4x4. "Be right back."

I walked briskly around the corner, out of sight, where I found the machine as described. Hundreds of people milled up and down the street, in and out of shops and stalls, practically shoulder to shoulder.

The ATM took my card but, like many I'd encountered, it had a small transaction limit: 800 cedis, or about US$200. I stuck my card back in, making multiple transactions, while it slowly dispensed the entire amount in grimy 20-cedi notes. By the time I had withdrawn several thousand cedis, people on the street were staring at this foreigner with a growing mountain of cash in his hands.

A man tapped me on the shoulder, and I looked up at a well-armed bank security guard.

"Is everything okay, sir?" he asked.

"Yes, fine!" I said. "But you don't have a plastic bag, by any chance?"

Unsmiling, he produced a black garbage sack from one pocket.

"Thanks a lot," I said gratefully, and stuffed the piles of notes inside.

Feeling like a drug dealer, I walked back around the corner and handed the heavy bag to Kalu.

"This is all yours," I said. "It should keep us going for a while. Just don't spend it all in one place!"

"Thanks," Kalu said, and hid the cash under his passenger seat. Then he straightened up and said, "Hey, Noah, I want to introduce you to my friend Cobby. We just bumped into each other on the street while you were at the ATM."

"Oh!" I said, suddenly aware that another man, a little shorter than Kalu and wearing a polo shirt, was standing next to us. "Hi, Cobby. Good to meet you."

As we shook hands, Kalu explained that Cobby Kwabena Tawiah had lately become interested in birds.

"Birdwatching is a great activity," Cobby said. "Kalu told me all about your trip, and I am very envious of your journey. I hope you have a good experience here in Ghana."

"Yes, we have already seen some amazing birds!" I said. "This morning on the Kakum walkway was incredible."

"I am glad to hear it," Cobby said. "I should really be going. It's good to see you, Kalu, and safe travels." He walked away and disappeared into the crowd.

Kalu and I climbed into the 4x4 and, mission accomplished, drove out of Cape Coast. As we navigated through traffic, Kalu said, "I am glad to see that Cobby is okay, because he recently had a frightening experience while watching birds."

"What happened?" I asked.

"Two weeks ago, Cobby was exploring by himself in a remote area, looking for new birding spots," Kalu said, "when he was suddenly surrounded by people from a nearby village who demanded to know what he was doing. They didn't believe his explanation about watching birds, which just made them more suspicious."

One of these villagers, Kalu told me, had accused Cobby of being "a kidnapper," and pretty soon a hysterical mob had formed, wielding machetes and sticks. Cobby calmly answered their questions: he was carrying a Swiss Army knife on his belt to cut vines and protect himself from animals, not as a weapon. And no, he hadn't asked the village chief for permission to walk there.

"You're a kidnapper!" the mob shouted, and they gave him three choices: either kill him on the spot, take him to their chief, or go to the police to settle the matter. Cobby picked the third option, but the villagers decided to go to their chief instead.

When the chief heard Cobby's side of the story, he was suspicious, too. So the chief issued a challenge: to prove that he was a birdwatcher, Cobby must produce three people within a half-hour who could vouch for him. Otherwise, he would be lynched as a kidnapper.

Fortunately, Cobby had cell service and, with the villagers watching closely, he called the Hans Cottage Botel near Kakum National Park, where a friend answered, and he explained the situation. Two people there headed out immediately while somebody else called Cobby's wife, telling her to call the police and hurry along, too.

When all of these people converged on the village, the police were angry and wanted to arrest the chief.

"But I am the one who just saved this man's life!" protested the chief. "I gave him a chance to prove himself!"

And so Cobby escaped a near-death experience.

Kalu said that when Cobby got home he was pretty shaken up. "I went to his house to console him and offer sympathy. See, I told him — birdwatching isn't easy!"

"Wow," I said. "That's quite a story."

"It is one of the dangers of exploring new territory," Kalu mused. "I've had similar experiences in Ghana, but less scary."

He laughed.

"That kind of thing would never happen in Nigeria, by the way," he said. "In Nigeria, people leave strangers alone. Because they don't know you, you might be anyone — even an angel — and it would be terrible to be responsible for harming an angel. The women will take turns cooking for you near their homes, for fear of interfering with something they don't understand. Nigerians treat themselves and their friends in all kinds of ways, but they are very afraid of being inhospitable to strangers."

✦-✦-✦

Kalu and I spent the last day of June at Mole (pronounced MOH-lay) National Park, in the interior of Ghana. The landscape at Mole is classic Africa — flat, dry, thorny — and here, after a week in dense rainforest, I caught my first snatches of some of the continent's better-known creatures.

The Mole Motel, where most visitors stay, is perched on a sweeping escarpment overlooking a waterhole. First thing in the morning, when I stepped bleary-eyed outside my room, I nearly knocked into a passing baboon. Vervet monkeys, warthogs, and kob (a deerlike animal) prowled the hotel's grounds.

"This place looks like a movie set!" I said.

"No, you've got it backwards," Kalu replied. "The movies are supposed to look like this."

The two of us were joined by a park guard named Robert Tindana, dressed head to toe in green khaki and outfitted with a rifle, and a friend of Kalu's named Ziblim Illiasu. At twenty-eight, Illiasu was less than a year younger than me and had been birding for about three years, partly inspired by Kalu.

"It makes you crazy," Illiasu said, when I asked him why he liked watching birds. "And it's such an adventure!"

He told me that he had never met another birder his own age.

"This is very inspiring for me," he said, wonderingly. "I thought they were all really old."

After a quick breakfast, we all crowded into Yaw's 4x4 pickup for a full morning on the park lands. Red dirt roads spidered into the bush. Kalu picked a route that looped between several waterholes and an area of dry flats, where he hoped to find a few specialties.

Birds abounded: bushshrikes, babblers, and sunbirds sang from the scrub; a Rose-ringed Parakeet flew over; and African Palm-Swifts fluttered against the sky. We had great views of a pair of Oriole Warblers, their scalloped black heads contrasting with olive green bodies. At one small waterhole, a Lesser Moorhen — the only one I would see all year — emerged long enough to allow a close study of its yellow bill, distinguishing this bird from the much more widespread Eurasian Moorhen.

Almost every species was a lifer for me, and I did my best to keep up. Some names, like the Red-cheeked Cordonbleu — a tiny, pastel-blue songbird — were evocative, but others challenged the limits of memory. One family of drab skulkers, called cisticolas, was especially confusing: each species looked similarly brown, so they had all been named for their sounds. In Ghana I recorded Whistling, Winding, Zitting, Singing, Siffling, and Croaking, and that was just the beginning; I'd soon add the Trilling, Wailing, Piping, Chattering, Rattling, Wing-snapping, and Rock-loving Cisticolas, among a dozen other species. If Snow White's seven dwarves were born identical twins, they'd still be a cinch to keep straight by comparison.

Near the end of the morning, before returning to the hotel for lunch, we stopped at one last waterhole. Robert, the park guard, led us quietly through a stand of trees where the view opened into a wide, shallow lake.

I caught my breath. At the water's edge, like a living sculpture, stood two enormous African elephants — the first wild elephants I'd ever seen. They were just a few hundred yards away, facing us with long, curving tusks. One slowly filled its trunk and hosed gallons of water down its mouth, swishing its tail at the flies. They didn't seem to mind us watching from this distance, and we halted until the elephants moved off with slow, loping strides.

"Wow," I said. "For a minute, I forgot all about cisticolas!"

"Yes," Kalu laughed. "But, you know, we wouldn't have seen the elephants if we weren't looking for birds."

Robert explained that poaching is not a big issue at Mole National Park, partly because of regular guard patrols, and that these elephants live a relatively peaceful, unthreatened existence. Later, elsewhere in Africa and Asia, I'd see so many elephants that they would almost seem normal, but I luxuriated in this first encounter.

Illiasu and Robert bid goodbye after lunch, and Yaw, Kalu, and I hit the road again, heading south toward Accra. My week in Ghana was nearly finished. Tomorrow the calendar would flip to July. Exactly six months had passed since the New Year, and with half the world still ahead, I had seen 3,334 species of birds, including nearly 300 new ones in Ghana. If I maintained this pace, I would surely exceed my goal of 5,000.

For now, I settled down to watch the colors of west Africa slide past in a vivid stream: red dust, black soot, flowery dresses, straw-yellow roofs, green foliage, bowls of ripe fruit balanced on shaven heads. Judging by the roadside shops, Ghana was quite a God-fearing country. As we drove through a city called Kumasi, I noted the Saint Computer Service, By His Grace Phones, With God Carpentry Works Shop, God Is in Control Sewing and Decoration, the Sweet Mother Bar, and — leaving nothing to chance — the Holy Driving Institute. I pointed out a store called the Nothing But Christ Electrical Shop to Kalu.

"Do you go to church?" I asked. "It looks like the faith is strong here."

"Of course!" he said. "Most of my family are born-again Christians, but some of them keep the old ways. I myself believe in voodoo and magic."

"Really?" I asked, intrigued. "Like what?"

"I have seen things," Kalu said. "For instance, one time I saw an empty boat on the earth with a man standing next to it, making paddling motions with his hands. The boat moved on its own — that was magic."

He went on to explain that, living in Accra, he had to attend church so people wouldn't think he was too weird for being a birder.

"I just don't like hearing about hell and everything all the time," he said. "I want to die quietly one day and rest in peace. So, as a compromise, I joined a Mormon church and have been going there every Sunday for years."

"Is that much different than other churches?" I asked.

"Oh, yes," Kalu said. "The Mormons don't have dancing, partying, and endless sermons — a man just tells us calm things each week. By the end of the service, I am so relaxed! They don't yell in my face, or force me to give money."

His friends, he added, often asked about these services; they would see people go in but couldn't hear any drums or singing.

"People wonder what happens inside, because it doesn't seem much like church to them," he said.

Kalu asked politely if I was religious.

"I don't go to church, if that's what you mean," I said. "But I believe in the power of nature. Everything is connected, and we are all part of a larger whole. For me, I guess watching birds is as much a religious experience as listening to a preacher. Birds can teach us a lot about the world and our place in it."

"Amen," Kalu said.

A minute later, just beyond the Blood of Jesus Sewing Center and the End Time Cold Store, I saw a strange vision: a full-grown man stood tall on the roadside, facing traffic, without a stitch of clothing. The naked man stared at us, his eyes widening when we passed.

"Whoa, did you see that?" I exclaimed.

"Yes," Kalu said. "That was a madman."

Then he flashed a mischievous smile.

"In Ghana," he said, "we have a saying that might as well apply to birders: not all madmen are naked!"

12

The Karamoja Apalis

IN BIRDWATCHING, size doesn't really matter. That is, the length of a life list does not necessarily measure the caliber of its author. In fact, the opposite is often true: you can build a big list by seeking new birds instead of observing the same birds repeatedly — as many of the world's top listers do — but the result is that you'll have only a passing understanding of what you have seen, in the same way that someone who spends an hour at John F. Kennedy International Airport in New York City watches a lot of planes but can't possibly grasp all the nuances of the city's culture. It takes time to get to know birds, and time is a luxury that often goes by the wayside in the listing game.

Expertise comes from focusing on a single region or taxonomic group, or even just one species. There is no such thing as "the greatest birder in the world" — and even if such a determination could be made, it probably wouldn't be the guy with the most notches on his binocs, me included.

Here's an example. A couple of years ago, I took

part in an organized group tour of Ecuador for a few days. The trip was led by one of the country's most experienced guides, who had an encyclopedic knowledge of the 1,700 species found there. Several of the tour's participants had recorded many more birds than that — one man had a life list approaching 8,000 — but when I asked them about certain species, they couldn't remember them without checking a spreadsheet. The guide pointed out every single bird. He set up a spotting scope and people lined up to peer through it, hardly bothering to try spotting birds on their own. The best birder in this group wasn't one of the high listers; it was the guide, who had spent a lifetime studying the birds of one country.

So what does a list measure, if not expertise or talent? Some argue that a list is only a metric of the depth of one's pockets and the free time to empty them. Those critics have a point, but I think a list is grander than that: besides reflecting how many places a person has traveled, it measures the desire to see those places and those birds firsthand. A list, in other words, is a personal account of dreams and memories. It conveys poetry and passion and inspiration.

+ – + – +

My year list was growing by leaps and bounds, but in Africa I started to lose my grip. Everywhere else, I'd had at least a basic knowledge of the birds in each region, but here, on the one continent I'd never touched before, everything was brand-new. I traveled too fast to prepare thoroughly, which meant that I was forced to learn the birds as I went. My capacity for absorbing names and field marks was stretched to the limit.

With Kalu's guidance, I encountered a total of 318 bird species in just over a week in Ghana, 295 of which I'd never seen before in my life. Learning the bird names became an all-consuming task. I mixed up my cisticolas; I confused my camaropteras and eremomelas; I puzzled over the Copper-tailed Starling and Bronze-tailed Starling.

Typically, for long-distance birding trips, I study for months in advance. To know what to expect, there is no substitute for home-work — poring through field guides, listening to tapes, reading trip reports, printing out checklists, and researching locations. Then, when I land in a new place, I have a map in my head of what I'm looking for, ready for the treasure hunt.

Now, though, I struggled to keep up. Studying the birds of one country is different than taking on the whole planet. It wasn't pos-sible to know every bird ahead of time, so I did my best to figure out the African species along the way. By the time I left the continent two months later, I'd have a pretty good handle on its bird life, but the first forays were overwhelming.

My strategy of connecting with locals really paid off in unfa-miliar surroundings. In Africa I depended heavily on the expertise of my hosts. Some were full-time guides, others had day jobs, still others were students, and a few were retired, but they all had one thing in common: they lived there, and they were willing to share with me their sheer love of birds. This network of birders literally meant the world to me. Without it, I would have found fewer spe-cies, made fewer friends, learned less about each place, and had a lot less fun.

The purist, hoping to level birding's playing field, might sug-gest that guides shouldn't be allowed on listing endeavors at all — that any bird first spotted by someone else shouldn't count. As appealing as it sounds, the logic of this idea quickly breaks down, and not just because it ignores the camaraderie that is such a huge part of the enjoyment of birdwatching. I once thought that a "self-found" Big Year would be a noble enterprise, but gradually real-ized that imposing this limitation would be a recipe for ignorance and loneliness of planetary proportions. Refusing to use guides is like starting a business without an accountant, or writing a book without an editor: it suggests that you'd rather be incompetent than learn from others.

Still, I generally avoided group tours of the sort I once experienced in Ecuador. It would have been easy enough — though way beyond the modest book advance that was financing this trip — to contact one or two international bird-tour businesses and have them arrange everything. Several excellent companies advertise birding trips on all seven continents, with stables of expert leaders, efficient office staff, and knowledgeable ground agents. They are happy to craft bespoke itineraries, and some will even rustle up tourmates if you don't have a vanful of friends.

But my Big Year wouldn't work with the usual birding-tour strategy. For one thing, I had specific and sometimes unusual targets in each destination, skipping the birds I'd already seen. I had to move fast — on average, twice as quickly as organized tours do. Though it sounds strange, I also had to miss a lot of birds, an approach that champion birder Stuart Keith once aptly called "worldwide cream-skimming." Finally, for the kind of journey I envisioned, it just didn't seem appropriate to use big companies. I wanted one-on-one time with local characters and visionaries in far-flung places, and I was willing to sacrifice a few species for the sake of that. I knew I couldn't live like a local while surrounded by other foreigners on pre-packaged tours, so I made a rule from the start: all of my guides had to live in the country where I joined them.

The grassroots strategy worked better than I had dared hope, and I stuck to it through virtually the entire year. I scheduled only two group tours, in South Africa and Tanzania, to save money: in both cases, companions would dramatically reduce the cost of exploring the big national parks, which were geared toward groups on safari. I'd still have local guides but would be joined by other birders on each leg — several independent travelers in South Africa and a group of American friends in Tanzania — for a more formal tour experience. In these places, for the first time this year, I'd be part of a lister crowd. I just hoped they could keep pace.

My mid-July arrival in South Africa came at 1 a.m. on a redeye from Cameroon to Johannesburg. Throughout seventeen days in the West African wet season, in a wide river of humanity, I'd seen exactly two other white people — a pair of missionaries in a remote village in Ghana — and it felt strange to be surrounded by white faces. Was this reverse culture shock? I'd gotten so used to being a minority that I only noticed when I no longer stuck out.

The past nine days in Cameroon had been an intense journey into the heart of darkness. I'd seen some amazing birds, including an odd species called a Gray-necked Rockfowl, which attaches its mud nest to the vertical walls of rainforest caves. And I'd witnessed wonderful places, from the coast to the misty slopes of Mount Cameroon, the tallest mountain in West Africa. But conditions in Cameroon were challenging and dispiriting. When I arrived, the man I'd contacted, Benji — the only local birder I could find in all of Cameroon — told me he'd spent the expense money I wired ahead without making any reservations for us, and he asked for a loan to cover our trip, which he never paid back. A large man without front teeth, Benji said between cigarettes that tourism had crashed in Cameroon after Boko Haram guerrillas invaded the northern part of the country, and that he was surviving by selling knickknacks at a botanical garden in Douala. I felt sorry for him, but also chagrined that he'd applied my entire Cameroon budget to his personal debts.

The roads, muddy from monsoon rains, were a nightmare. We had breakdowns, delays, detours, more breakdowns, and more delays. I slept in buildings that in other countries would have been condemned; most had no other guests. For the better part of nine days we got along with no electricity, running water, or toilet paper while eating everything — mostly rice and goat meat for breakfast, lunch, and dinner — with our hands. Washing clothes was out of the question, so the whole time I wore the same mud-and-sweat-soaked shirt and pants, which in the heavy humidity never dried out. Birding in Cameroon is hard enough without trying to do it on a shoestring during the wet season, and it was heartbreaking to know that despite all our efforts I missed a lot of birds. I left Douala while heavy rains flooded the city; my last memory is of an outdoor market where sellers and customers sloshed around in three feet of water and mud. Four months later, in October, hundreds of U.S. troops deployed to north Cameroon to help fight the guerrillas in what would become a long and indeterminate occupation.

I caught a little sleep on the floor of the Johannesburg airport before Wayne Jones, the leader of my South African tour, appeared in crisp attire and a clean white van to pick me up at 6 a.m. The other five participants had arrived the previous day and were waking up at a nearby hotel. Appraising my ragged appearance, Wayne said, "Let's get you to the hotel to freshen up — you can grab a quick shower there before we head out."

"Is there hot running water?" I asked.

"Of course — it's a hotel!" Wayne said.

For once, I was glad to be on an organized tour. The constant struggle of Cameroon had worn me down, and I needed a mental break. For this South African stretch, I wouldn't have to worry about anything except finding birds. The tour had been organized by Rockjumper, the world's biggest birding tour operator (by set departures), which is headquartered in Johannesburg. I couldn't wait to relax a little and hang out with a convivial group of birders.

Soaping up in the gloriously steamy shower, I wondered who they might be.

Wayne, tall and slender with short hair and a craggy smile, lived in Johannesburg and worked full-time leading tours for Rock-jumper. After this tour he'd be headed straight to Namibia, rotating with other assignments in places like Ethiopia, Kenya, and India. We were now in his home territory: eastern South Africa, home of Kruger National Park and all its natural wonders.

As Wayne drove the van, I gradually got to know the rest of the group: Martha Miller (a curriculum specialist) and Janine Gregory (an economist) from Canada; Brian Rapoza (an environmental teacher) and Alan Mitchnick (a biologist) from the United States; and Klas Magnus Karlsson, a quirky high school physics teacher from Sweden and my roommate for the week. Janine had been talked into the trip by Martha on the strength of cute safari animals, but the rest of us were serious birders.

We were all excited for what the next few days would bring. Kruger National Park, on the border with Mozambique and Zimbabwe, is the size of Israel. More than five hundred species of birds have been recorded within its borders, but the park is famed for hosting the "big five," supposedly the most difficult African animals to hunt — the lion, leopard, elephant, buffalo, and rhinoceros — along with other safari creatures: cheetah, zebra, giraffe, wildebeest, hippo, hyena, impala, rhebok, steenbok, blesbok, eland, kudu, hartebeest, suni, topi, oribi, duiker, nyala, sitatunga, klipspringer. This is South Africa's flagship reserve, visited by more than a million tourists a year, outfitted with two dozen safari lodges and hundreds of park rangers. At night everyone must stay within designated camps surrounded by high fences — if you're not back by 5:30 p.m., you'll pay a stiff fine — and then the park becomes a reverse zoo, with free-roaming animals surrounding the locked-up humans.

And birds! Some, like the Southern Ground-Hornbill and Kori Bustard, are as big and charismatic as the furry animals. Birds of the African savanna are relatively easy to see; if South America, with its thousands of species, is known as "the bird continent," then Africa is "the bird watching continent" for its raw spectacle. On safari, you don't have to spend hours stalking cryptic species through slimy jungles, because the birds sit in plain view.

Kruger's park rules forbid people to exit their vehicles lest a predator suddenly leap from the bushes, so everyone drives slowly around a network of one-lane roads, circling like the White-backed Vultures that soar overhead. As Wayne piloted our van into the park, we leapfrogged between traffic jams with good results: at one group of cars, a pride of lions emerged from the bush within spitting distance, and at another pile-up a zebra carcass seethed in scavenging hyenas and jackals. A passerby rolled down his window to direct us to a nearby group of white rhinos. Later, joining three other cars at a wide pullout, we watched two leopards lounging in the grass, barely visible on a hidden sandbank.

Each time we stopped, other vehicles appeared behind our van's bumper, their occupants straining to see what we'd spotted. It was like pointing at the sky on a crowded street — pretty soon everyone is looking up. As soon as Wayne hit the brakes five cars would stack up behind us, hoping we'd spotted a big cat. When they realized it was just a dove, or a kingfisher, most people drove off, embarrassed or annoyed, as if they'd been duped. Eventually, we hit on a solution that worked pretty well: whenever anyone got close, one of us rolled down the window and flashed a copy of *Birds of South Africa*. We called this ploy "flipping them the bird."

Never mind the big animals, the birding was fantastic. Flocks tumbled through the bushveld, and whenever our group came across one of these concentrations chaos erupted inside the van.

"Green-winged Pytilia!" shouted Wayne, stopping abruptly on

a desolate stretch of dirt road. "Look for the little red-and-green bird on the ground, just underneath the shrubs on the left."

"I see a Chinspot Batis, too!" Alan added.

"Oh, what's that bird next to the batis?" exclaimed Martha. "It's bright orange-yellow underneath!"

"Sulphur-breasted Bushshrike," Wayne said. "Does everybody see it?"

I found myself wondering how I could get more excited about a Cape Crombec — a beige-gray bird less than five inches long — than a whole herd of zebras, and remembered something Kalu had said in Ghana: "We wouldn't have seen the elephants if we weren't looking for birds." His words resonated more deeply the more I considered them.

My year list was helping me appreciate our Earth at different scales. Sometimes it's easier to absorb a large canvas, like Kruger, by examining it one small detail at a time — the difference between breezing through an art exhibit and stopping to ponder each piece. I felt more intimately connected to this landscape through the intricate plumage of a Miombo Wren-Warbler than the sight of a thousand wildebeest, because the wren-warbler required closer attention. This pursuit of birds, with prolonged focus and effort, was like a portal to the world, from the tiniest detail to the biggest panorama.

In a park full of tourists on safari, I was glad to be in a group of birders. All day we discussed nothing but our shared obsession. Nobody called us idiosyncratic for traveling halfway around the world, to one of the most spectacular big-game wildlife extravaganzas, to stare at diminutive petronias and tit-flycatchers. Cocooned inside the van with Wayne at the wheel and a nonstop stream of birds outside, we were fully immersed. If a flow state is bliss, then in this company I experienced pure contentment.

Later, adding up the day's sightings, I discovered that the Gray

Go-away-bird (named for its "Go 'way!" catcall) was bird number 3,500 — a new milestone, and I hadn't even realized it! That number hardly captured the thrill of exploring Kruger National Park with a van of happy birders. It was true that my list motivated me to explore the world and measure progress, but the list itself was no more descriptive than a phone book — a crude proxy for riches beyond numbers or words.

In late August, in northern Tanzania, I wrapped up my African safari with several days in the Serengeti. The landscape here is much different than the bushveld of South Africa: wide open plains, baobabs, silhouetted acacias, the kind of long vistas where your eyes can get lost with your soul. East Africa is deservedly famous for its savannas, and the Serengeti epitomizes this landscape — in the local Maasai language, the word means "the place where the land runs on forever." The Serengeti's reputation can transcend even its own expanse: in a list compiled by *USA Today* and *Good Morning America*, it was chosen as one of the "New Seven Wonders of the World," alongside polar ice caps, Mayan ruins, and "the Internet."

By now I was on a first-name basis with the African megafauna. I had spent the past couple weeks in South Africa, birding first with Wayne Jones and then for a few days around Cape Town and the Western Cape with two sharp young birders, Ethan Kistler and Callan Cohen. I followed that with a great run in Madagascar, with Jacky Ratiantsihoarana, and in Kenya with a bird expert named Joseph Aengwo. Now, in Tanzania, I was joined by three friends from Oregon who hadn't yet experienced a full-on safari: Harv Schubothe, Kelle Herrick, and David Heath. The four of us met a local birder named Anthony Raphael and a driver, Roger Msengi, who packed us into a modified Land Cruiser, and our group rolled straight toward the Serengeti.

It was a relief that everyone had arrived OK. To help share the costs of the Land Cruiser, driver, and accommodations, I had recruited other birders for this leg — the only place where I went out of my way to sign up birding companions — and was delighted that the three Oregonians had agreed to come along. But when I wired thousands of dollars for the trip months ahead of time, a hacker cleverly diverted the funds to an account in Uganda. I never got the money back despite an extended bank investigation. The Tanzania outfitter's ground agent sent me a series of messages admitting that the company's email had been hacked, unfortunately, but blamed me for sending the money to the wrong place and insisted that I wire more (to their proper account this time) or the trip would be canceled. The whole costly business left such a bad taste that I would have canceled if I hadn't already convinced three of my friends to join me.

As it turned out, maybe I should have canceled anyway.

The reason was serious: after a productive stretch elsewhere in South and East Africa, I had just about run out of birds. With a sinking heart, I realized that I'd already seen almost all of the northern Tanzania species in Kenya and other countries. The bird life of East Africa had seemed so diverse that, when plotting my route, I hadn't thought twice about scheduling weeks here. Now, locked into a twelve-day trip, it was obvious that the pace of new sightings would dramatically slow down. There was nothing I could do about it.

Such is the tradeoff of planning ahead: a fully booked itinerary allows more time in the field instead of working out the logistics en route, but it also permits less flexibility. For the most part, I was committed to arrangements I'd made nearly a year ago, before leaving home. Back then, lacking a blueprint or optimal schedule to follow, I had laid out a logical route based on my best guess. During the Big Year, as I was learning, I couldn't easily change plans without letting people down, and I was keenly aware that many local birders had gone out of their way to give their time as guides and hosts. If I'd badly overestimated my time in Tanzania, I would just have to make the most of it.

As the days progressed, the number of new species dwindled. In twelve days in Tanzania, I found only 80 new birds — on several days, just one — dragging down my daily average for the year. Nonetheless, I hit a huge milestone — my 4,000th species, a Mountain Gray Woodpecker in a shade-grown coffee plantation — and savored the sights and sounds of this beautiful country. Tanzania abounds in big wildlife and landscapes, from the Ngorongoro Crater — by some measures, the world's largest caldera — to Mount Kilimanjaro, the highest mountain in Africa. The actual Serengeti was like a movie of itself: the place where millions of wildebeest migrate across crocodile-infested rivers, the land that inspired *The Lion King*, and the home of Maasai warriors. Fossils discovered near Serengeti National Park suggest that some of the first humans lived on this spot. Two million years later, this landscape remains timeless.

The bird I got most excited about in Tanzania was the Karamoja Apalis. The name evokes nothing for most people, perhaps not even for most birders, and that's exactly why I wanted to see one: it's a birder's bird, an aficionado's tick. In a country with a reputation for large wildlife, I held out for a tiny, obscure creature.

The Karamoja Apalis is quite small, less than five inches long including a slender tail, and weighs less than two nickels. It's not much to look at, pale gray above and whitish below, with white patches on the wings and a diminutive bill. It vaguely resembles a New World gnatcatcher and is somewhat related, though the Apalis genus is closer to the cisticola family. But whatever the bird's shortcomings in appearance, it makes up for with rarity. This species is one of Africa's most range-restricted birds, known from only a few sites in Uganda (in the Karamoja region), south Kenya, and northern Tanzania, where it is confined to patches of whistling thorn woodland. It wasn't found in the Serengeti until the 1990s and is still hard to see; to encounter one, you must know where to look.

We set out for an eventful morning on the Serengeti Plains. In short order, our group found a leopard up a tree, a cheetah on a kill, and a pack of thirteen lions napping in the shade of an isolated acacia tree. To see the three big cats in one session was quite a trick, and I was as excited as everyone else (I counted twenty-seven safari vehicles parked bumper-to-bumper at the lion spot), but we were on the lookout for birds, too. I added several new species before lunch, including a Fischer's Lovebird, Red-throated Tit, and Temminck's Courser — an odd species of big-eyed, droopy-billed shorebird that prefers to nest on freshly burned grassland.

In the afternoon, after a quick stop at a picnic area where Gray-headed Social-Weavers nested in a small colony, Anthony suggested we try for the apalis.

"It's in a more remote section of the park," he said, "away from most of the tourists."

"That sounds great!" I said, and Harv, Kelle, and David readily agreed.

"We can see other birds along the way," Anthony said, "but the apalis is the main target."

Roger navigated our open-roofed Land Cruiser down a series of dusty dirt tracks, occasionally crossing streams and shoving through thorny acacia limbs, while tsetse flies — the big, blood-sucking insects responsible for transmitting African *trypanosomiasis*, better known as sleeping sickness — swarmed around us. The tsetses were slow and easy to swat, though one managed to crawl up my pant leg and chomp down. It felt like a horsefly bite. When I reflexively smacked it, the fly's body exploded, smearing my pants with blood. Contracting sleeping sickness in Tanzania carries a low risk, but I didn't want to push my luck; the disease involves a brain parasite that, left untreated, results in neurological symptoms and eventually death.

It took half the afternoon to reach Anthony's stakeout. By the time Roger stopped our Land Cruiser and turned off the engine, we hadn't seen another vehicle in hours, which made a nice change. We disembarked next to a patch of thorny forest and began to look for little gray birds.

The Karamoja Apalis prefers whistling thorn, a type of acacia tree that grows in sparse woodlands. This tree produces hollow, gourdlike thorns, which are occupied by symbiotic ants that help defend against herbivores. Because appropriate stands of whistling thorn are found only in places with the right soil, the apalis has a very limited range.

Finding this bird is mostly a matter of tracking down the right habitat. Once on the scene, it didn't take us long to spot a Karamoja Apalis — species number 4,028 — flitting among thorny branches. I snapped a few photos, put my camera down, and watched for a while as it grabbed several small insects, probing delicately, somehow managing not to skewer its eyeballs on the thorns.

This bird was a real find, but greater satisfaction came the next day, when I signed the guest book at one of the park lodges. Flipping through the pages, all the notable sightings seemed to revolve around lions, leopards, and cheetahs, punctuated by the occasional hyena or elephant encounter. I didn't even hesitate. In block caps, I wrote "KARAMOJA APALIS!!!!!" and went away with a grin stretching from one ear to the other.

On the way back to Arusha I slouched next to Harv while Roger drove. Anthony occupied his usual spot in the passenger seat, and Kelle was in the back. David had left us to take a separate transport for Pemba Island, waving goodbye as he hopped into a different vehicle. As we drove along a deserted stretch of straight, paved highway that afternoon, we jabbered happily about our latest sightings and looked forward to the next stops.

In an instant, with a sound like a cannon blast, the back right tire of the Land Cruiser blew out at seventy miles per hour and the vehicle, shuddering violently, left the pavement. It happened too fast for me to process, except that Harv and I hung on to each other as we hit the ditch. Roger didn't try to swerve; instead, he guided us across the opposing lane, down an embankment, and into the bush alongside the road, where we came to rest in a cloud of dust. Luckily there was nothing to hit and no traffic.

After a shaky moment, all of us climbed out to inspect the exploded tire, a heavy model designed for off-roading. Harv and Kelle hugged.

"I'm glad you're okay, buddy," Harv said to me.

We were a silent and sober bunch. I couldn't help thinking what might have happened if not for Roger's capable hands at the wheel.

Within a few minutes Roger had replaced the tire. We were off again, the near-miss receding behind us, and the next bird somewhere ahead on the long Serengeti horizon.

13

A New World Record

ON AUGUST 23, while I was in northern Tanzania, a new post appeared on the website of Arjan Dwarshuis, the Dutch birder who had announced months earlier his aim to travel the world for a Big Year in 2016. I had periodically checked Arjan's blog since learning about him from Gunnar Engblom in Peru in March, but aside from a couple of minor clarifications, Arjan hadn't posted much. The last update on his site was more than three months old when this new post popped up.

"I've been very busy with planning my world big year," he began, "and I am very, very pleased to say that the flights for the first three months are booked!"

He added that he'd convinced friends to join him for parts of his trip, and that he was looking forward to getting started in a few months. The next paragraph snapped me to attention.

"As Noah Strycker is doing extremely well on his world big year and will surely set an incredible, very hard to beat record, I had to step up my game," Arjan wrote. "And so I did . . ."

The post went on to explain, in detail, Arjan's projected Big Year itinerary, set to begin the instant mine ended, at midnight on December 31. My jaw dropped as I read further. He had scrapped his original twenty-three-country map in favor of a route remarkably similar to mine: in all of South, Central, and North America, he now listed exactly the same countries I had visited, with added layovers in Suriname, the Dominican Republic, and Cuba. His route was also similar in Africa and Asia, tweaked here and there to squeeze out a few more birds; most of the differences involved cutting adventurous destinations (Antarctica, Cameroon, Myanmar) and streamlining the number of days in places where I'd seen fewer species. Just like me, he announced that he would travel continuously for the whole year, contribute to a carbon offset program, track his sightings on an Internet database, and post regular updates with a blog. It was like reading about my own project through the words of someone else!

Should I be flattered, uneasy, or excited by this development? I wasn't sure. One thing was certain, though: I had some serious competition. Arjan would follow a bird taxonomy favored by Europeans, different from the Clements Checklist that I was using on eBird, so he would play literally by different rules and could count a couple hundred species not recognized by Clements. Also, with a leap year, he would have an extra day. But his biggest advantage, I reflected, would be the benefit of hindsight. Having watched my whole effort unfold, he could learn from my successes and mistakes, and he clearly meant to go after whatever record I set.

Ah, well, I thought, you never can tell what the future will bring. If this guy was inspired to repeat my quest, so much the better — it would focus more attention on the world of birds and birding. Maybe we would even cross paths somewhere.

But that was getting way ahead of things — I hadn't even reached the record yet myself! As September approached, my time in Africa was winding down. After Tanzania, I spent twelve days in Uganda, where a phenomenal birder named Livingstone Kalema helped me track down 517 species of birds — including one of the country's most-wanted birds, a Green-breasted Pitta, in the wild tangles of vines and greenery of the Kibale Forest, and incidentally my very first pitta. When I left Africa, my Big Year totaled more than 4,200, inching closer to the 4,341 species mark set in 2008 by the British couple, Ruth Miller and Alan Davies. They sent a nice message on Facebook when I was within striking distance: "Hi Noah, you are going like a train! Congrats. You must be on for 5,000 plus?"

With four months remaining, I was pretty sure of reaching my goal of 5,000 species, but I couldn't afford to slack off — not with somebody ready to challenge any bar I set — and I began to feel the first vague stirrings of a possible 6,000 species by year's end. For now, I'd be satisfied with a new world record. Looking east, I set my sights on Asia.

The people of India are record fanatics. About 10 percent of all Guinness World Records applications come from India, and the country has its own set of record books: The *India Book of Records*, not to be confused with the *Indian Achiever Book of Records* or the *Limca Book of Records*. Indians go to extraordinary lengths to be recognized by these authorities — sometimes literally, like the man who hasn't cut his fingernails since 1952 or the one with the Guinness record for longest ear hair (5.19 inches).

On the whole planet, I couldn't pick a better place than India to set a Big Year world record, and it looked like that was just where it would happen. When I landed at Cochin International Airport in Kochi on September 13, in the bird-rich south India province of Kerala, my list stood at 4,243 species, just 98 short of Ruth and Alan's total. With more than a thousand species of birds to choose from in India, 80 percent of which I hadn't yet seen, I figured I would pass that number within a week.

For most of this year, I hadn't dwelt on breaking the existing record, as my goal from the outset was to see 5,000 species, half of the birds on Earth — a nice, round, individual challenge, not measured against the efforts of others. This was such an intensely personal quest that I hated to define it by someone else's idea of success; birding, after all, is not usually a competitive activity.

But a Big Year is still a competition, and as I edged closer to the world record I couldn't stop thinking about it. Buzz was building, too, with an upsurge of visits and comments on my daily blog at Audubon.org, messages of encouragement on my Facebook page, updates and discussions on online birding forums around the world, and requests for interviews from home and abroad. I responded as best I could, but it was hopeless; I couldn't keep up with the virtual world while living so large in the real world.

Actual and virtual reality intersected briefly in an unexpected way just before I arrived in India, during a day of birding squeezed into a layover in the United Arab Emirates. Two top-notch birders — Mark Smiles and Oscar Campbell — kindly showed me around the sand deserts on the outskirts of Abu Dhabi and Dubai while we baked in a slow oven of hundred-degree heat. The three of us found well over a hundred species of birds that day, including a rare find — a Green Warbler, crawling under a bush near an irrigated field, that was completely out of place, having been recorded in the UAE only about ten times.

The gilt-edged UAE made for a surreal layover, sandwiched between rural Uganda and India. I cast my eyes up, up, up the Burj Khalifa — the world's tallest building — while traveling on a twelve-lane freeway packed with luxury cars. As we watched the sun set over the Oman border fence that evening, Oscar mentioned that he'd just received an interesting email.

"Hey, some birder said he's doing a Big Year next year," he said, "with a goal of seeing five thousand species, just like you!"

"That wouldn't be Arjan, would it?" I asked.

"Yeah, that's his name," Oscar said. "Do you know him?"

"We haven't met," I said, "but I know who he is."

I had the increasing feeling that this Dutch guy was breathing down my neck — not just planning a similar adventure, but strategizing to go after me personally, and I had not even set a record yet! He was also starting to contact some of the same birders that I had connected with. In the UAE, of all places, people were saying hi to me for him. It was odd.

"Anyway," Oscar said, "you should have the world record wrapped up pretty soon."

"Yeah, but the record is sort of beside the point," I said, "though it will be satisfying to beat it. I'm still going for 5,000, which is a long way off."

"The record is important, though," Oscar said, "because people will get excited about it. All you have to say is that you broke a world record, and anyone can understand what that means, even if they have no idea what birding is."

He was right, of course. No matter what the original goal, all eyes — including mine — were now on the existing mark of 4,341 birds.

A couple days later I landed in the tea plantations of the Western Ghats mountain range, near the south Indian city of Munnar, with a gregarious birder named Harsha Jayaramaiah who seemed to know everybody in the country. He and his friends had generously organized among themselves to save money during my stay by sharing accommodations, food, and transportation. Their gift meant a lot to me, for it cut my total expenses to about $15 a day — the lowest of the whole year and well under my typical daily expenses of about $200 — while allowing me to enjoy the welcome hospitality of local birders. On my second day in India, I was just thirty-nine birds short of the record, which meant I'd probably pass it in another day or two. Harsha thought we might add a few more species in these mountains, including the Broad-tailed Grassbird — a skulky brown thing found only in grassy patches at high elevations in the Western Ghats. He couldn't locate a grassbird on short notice, though, so we stopped at a tourism office in Munnar for help.

Harsha asked to see a friend who knew about the bird, and sure enough, a man came out to give us some tips. When I thanked him, the man asked about my trip.

"Well, I hope to set a world record in the next day or so," I said, "for the number of birds anyone has ever seen in one year."

The man's face lit up like a light bulb.

"A world record?" he asked. "Are you going to submit it to the *Guinness Book of World Records*?"

"I did submit an official application, eight months ago," I said, "but I haven't heard back."

"That is strange," the man said. "They should reply in a few weeks."

"That's what the website says," I said, "but they can take as long as they want. Being in the Guinness book wasn't my main goal, anyway. I just want to see as many birds as I can."

"But how can you prove it?" the man pressed. "You will need evidence!"

"Birding doesn't really work like that — it's a personal adventure," I said, and the man looked dubious. "But I do have witnesses for every bird I've seen this year, and I've photographed a lot of them, too."

"Hmmph," he said, waggling his head. "Any record attempt must be documented. I had a friend who made it into the Guinness book earlier this year, and he had to provide all kinds of evidence."

"What was it for?" I asked.

The man glowed.

"Breaking iron rods with the bare fist!" he said, triumphantly.

It was obvious that he took this record very seriously. When Harsha and I left a few minutes later, on a mission to see the grassbird, the man was still sitting at his desk, fanning himself in the stuffy tourism office, lost in happy remembrance of his friend's colossal achievement.

World records carry the mystique of perfection — a Platonic ideal of the material world. They are easy to understand and elegantly simple. Logically, there can be only one largest animal (the blue whale) and lightest element (hydrogen). Everybody knows that Mount Everest is the tallest mountain on Earth, and the altitude of its summit — a somewhat random artifact of geology — is less significant for its exact elevation (29,029 feet) than as the ultimate benchmark against other lofty heights. Superlatives help define our universe by precisely measuring its outer limits, giving context for everything else.

For most of history, all world records were intrinsic: they existed, by virtue of physics or happenstance, whether or not anyone noticed. The world's oldest tree (a 5,062-year-old bristlecone pine in the White Mountains of California) didn't set out to achieve distinction; it has merely stood longer than any other tree. Likewise, the cheetah isn't consciously trying to be the fastest land animal when it sprints at speeds exceeding seventy miles per hour — it is more focused on its prey. Such records, born of chance or necessity, have little to do with recognition.

Only in recent years have people begun to equate world records with achievement. The notion of being the best is seductive, especially in an increasingly quantitative culture, and it's a quite modern concept. The ancient Olympic games originated as part of a religious festival honoring the Greek god Zeus, which went dormant in AD 393; their revival in 1896, more than 1,500 years later, dispensed with everything but unadulterated competition, leading to the multibillion-dollar spectacle we have today in which racewalkers and trampoliners are judged as solemnly as foreign policy. These days, we worship humans who run, jump, ride, swim, throw, wrestle, skate, ski, and curl better than other humans. It's not really logical, when you think about it: Michael Phelps and Usain Bolt are international celebrities, but the also-rans who finished a hundredth of a second behind them remain largely anonymous. And yet world records — or "WR," in Olympic parlance — are worth gold.

Practically speaking, our record-setting obsession aligns with two recent societal developments: enough leisure time to pursue non-survival-related activities, and the ability to know what other people are doing in distant places. It's hard to train for the decathlon if you work at a backbreaking job for eighteen hours a day, and equally difficult to proclaim a world champion without transcontinental communication.

Our greatest authority on world records started, according to legend, with a barroom dispute about birds. In the early 1950s, Sir Hugh Beaver, then the managing director of the Guinness Brewery, attended a shooting party in Ireland and got into an argument about which was the fastest game bird in Europe — he believed it was the golden-plover, but his friend maintained that the Red Grouse was speedier, and no reference could provide a definitive answer. Shortly afterward, Sir Hugh hired two journalists to research facts and figures for a collection of superlatives, first published as the *Guinness Book of Records* in 1955. The book quickly took on a life of its own; by 2015, *Guinness World Records* was the best-selling book of all time, with more than 100 million copies in print.

Sir Hugh Beaver intended his book as a reference, but it has morphed over time into a more interactive treasury. With no categorical restrictions imposed, people devised increasingly esoteric ideas, spurred on by the prospect of personal glory. Instead of describing the world as it is, the book has become the repository of humanity's sweeping desire to stand out from the crowd — a vision of the world as it might be, with sufficient ingenuity.

And so, while Guinness today lists the "fastest bird (diving)" as the Peregrine Falcon — once clocked in a stoop at 242 miles per hour — its database brims mostly with obscure human achievements. The latest triumphs are added in an endless, dizzying stream: largest display of origami elephants (78,564), most traffic cones balanced on the chin (26), largest sushi mosaic (608.16 square feet), and, my personal favorite, "most apples held in the mouth and cut by a chainsaw in one minute — self (blindfolded)," a terrifying stunt performed by an Australian man who calls himself The Space Cowboy. Each year, more than 50,000 people apply for new records.

I love all kinds of hijinks, but what does a world record mean when practically anything goes? Most people agree that running the fastest marathon is a stunning feat, but these other records, like hurling light bulbs or eating cars, are something else — a form of self-expression, perhaps. According to Guinness, each attempt must be measurable, verifiable, and breakable.

Searching for "bird" on Guinness's website returns more than 1,000 certified records, many of which are held by birds themselves: the Wild Turkey has the strongest gizzard, the Dusky Grouse has the shortest migration, and the Lake Duck of Argentina has the "largest reproductive organ for a bird" (its retractable spine-covered penis has been measured at 16.7 inches).

Birdwatching feats are conspicuously absent, probably because

Guinness considers them unverifiable. In my case, the Guinness Records Management Team sent their final decision nearly a year after I'd submitted my application: "Unfortunately, we are afraid to say that we cannot accept your proposal as a Guinness World Records title. Every record must be measurable and we feel that it would be difficult to provide an accurate measurement for your proposal."

This is why we have a Guinness record for the highest score on the Angry Birds video game, but nothing for those who pursue real, live birds.

Different people have their own reasons for striving toward a goal, and the psychology of record-setting is complicated. In a recent TED talk titled "The Puzzle of Motivation," viewed on YouTube nearly 20 million times, the analyst Dan Pink showed that external rewards have a surprisingly weak effect on all kinds of performance. After reviewing a pile of literature, Pink concluded that autonomy, mastery, and purpose — self-determination in the context of a larger focus — are much more powerful, and that real motivation comes from within. It's not the record that makes people pogo-stick up Mount Fuji, in other words; it's the personal desire to prove oneself and contribute to the world.

This is a subtly different way of viewing achievement that applies well to ambitious feats like Big Years: the end result may not be the reward, but the journey isn't exactly it, either. You need a goal, or at least a direction, to discover a true sense of purpose.

At least for me, journeys with a mission are far more rewarding — whether running a marathon or birding the world. It doesn't really matter what I'm seeking, only that I am inwardly driven to find it. Never was this truer than during my Big Year. My hope of seeing 5,000 species, and breaking the existing record in the process, motivated me to go out into the world, look for new birds every day, and celebrate and share what I found.

Two days later, on September 16, Harsha and I arrived at the That-tekad Bird Sanctuary, a lowland forest patch along the Periyar River, at first light. With twenty-seven species to go to the record, we met a local birder named Sanu Sasi, who knew the area's birds like the back of his hand. The three of us entered the sanctuary in lively spirits.

Soon after dawn, a convoy of vehicles pulled up: the Ezhu-punna Birders, a group of about a dozen young and enthusiastic bird lovers, had heard about my quest and wanted to help. They had driven two hours from the city of Kochi, having risen early to make the trip, and spilled out in a gaggle of smiles and hand-shakes.

With more than a dozen eager pairs of eyes in the forest, the birds had little chance of hiding. A Malabar Trogon, cherry red underneath with a black head and a thin white border encircling its neck, surveyed our group with apparent amusement from a high branch. Sanu pointed out a couple of Flame-throated Bulbuls, greenish yellow with black heads and orange throats, while Dark-fronted Babblers squeaked and rattled from the nearby under-growth. Several White-bellied Treepies, a flashy and long-tailed member of the crow family endemic to southern India, called nois-ily from the forest, eventually affording great views while crossing a gap between trees. The birding was so brisk that I could barely keep up, and the morning hours flew by with more than twenty new species.

By noon, I was counting down single digits: a tiny Heart-spot-ted Woodpecker, black and white with a spiky crest and practically no tail, put me within ten species of surpassing the record; and after several more sightings, a White-rumped Needletail, a type of swift, sliced the gap down to five. But then, with the record dangling so close, activity stalled. In early afternoon a discouraging, drizzling rain began to fall, birds stopped singing, and it seemed that we might not reach the hoped-for number that day after all.

The Ezhupunna Birders reluctantly clocked out for lunch, wishing luck to Harsha, Sanu, and me. With rain pounding, we held a quick strategy session under the shelter of a leaky, unoccupied hut. Sanu suggested that we look for some common water-loving species near his house a few miles away, so we spent the next couple of hours in a downpour, tramping back and forth across a grassy field; one by one, we managed to see a White-rumped Munia, a White-breasted Waterhen, and a flyover Gray-fronted Green-Pigeon, endemic to this part of India. Now I was one tantalizing species away from tying the world record.

"Hey, I just saw a Common Iora!" yelled Harsha, who was staring at a patch of low trees a couple hundred yards away. "Come on, I think it just zipped out the other side."

The three of us sloshed across the field to catch up with the bird, my heart pounding with excitement and exertion, but the iora — a sparrow-sized, yellowish green songbird with black-and-white wings — proved flitty and elusive. I couldn't get my eyes on it. We couldn't give up the search, even though it seemed a little ridiculous: the Common Iora is one of the most familiar bird species in India, yet right now it seemed like the single most important bird in the world.

Finally, after a frustrating half-hour of peekaboo, the iora danced onto a branch right in front of me, and Sanu, Harsha, and I splashed high fives.

"That ties the record of 4,341 birds," I said. "We just need one more to break it!"

Sanu and Harsha caught each other's eye.

"Yes, we've been saving one for you," Sanu said. "Come on, we will return to the Thattekad forest for your next species — it's a special one."

"Just don't look at anything else until we get there," Harsha said. "We don't want an unremarkable bird like the Common Iora to pass the world record!"

As we made the ten-minute drive back to the bird sanctuary, the rain lightened into swirling mist. I stared at my feet in the back seat, water puddling around my shoes, wondering what Sanu had staked out for us. Harsha called the Ezhupunna Birders, who had finished their lunch, and they met us at the entrance to the forest, along with several other people I didn't know, in anticipation of the big moment.

My stomach gnawed with hunger — I hadn't eaten all day — and my skin was soaked through, but none of that mattered. All I could think about was the imminent milestone. Here I was on Day 259 of my Big Year, a once-in-a-lifetime adventure that had already taken me on a splendid journey through Antarctica, South and Central America, the United States, Europe, Africa, and India. I still aimed for 5,000 birds, but hurdling over the world record was admittedly exciting. Heightened energy sparked in the air.

Sanu led the way into the forest on foot. At a spot where the trail crossed a small creek, he stopped quietly and gestured toward a dense group of trees.

"Do you see it?" he whispered.

"What?" I said. "A bird?"

Harsha laughed.

"It's no fair if we point it out," he said. "You have to find this one yourself!"

They eyed me while I scanned the thick foliage, my adrenaline kicking in. Nothing moved, not even a breath of wind. The air hung heavy, the light muted by an overhanging canopy and mist. What should I be looking for?

I felt the sense of being watched, and turned around to see . . . what was this? A TV camera and crew had somehow materialized out of nowhere.

"They're from an Indian news station," Harsha said, "and they want to show your expression when you see the record-breaking bird!"

Behind the camera crew loitered the Ezhupunna Birders and several others, all of them watching expectantly. That moment was so weird that I'll never forget it: about twenty people staring at me while I stared blankly into the trees, hoping to spot the bird that would officially break the record. Birdwatching is not usually a spectator sport.

Then I saw it: a clump of dead leaves that, on closer inspection, wasn't vegetative at all. I raised my binoculars with a sense of fate. Clinging to a horizontal branch in the midcanopy, partly obscured by foliage, a pair of bizarre-looking birds snuggled together. They were brown with rufous accents, fluffed out in a round ball, with their eyes squeezed shut and wings tucked into soft plumage; their heads were so large that they seemed not to have necks, and their bills were the same width. The effect suggested something between a decomposing clod and a plush toy.

"No way — it's a pair of Sri Lanka Frogmouths!" I exclaimed, with a huge grin. "They're roosting here for the day, aren't they?"

"Yes," Harsha said, as he grasped my arm. "The Sri Lanka Frogmouth is an excellent record-breaking bird, nocturnal and not easy to see! Lucky for us, Sanu knew where to find these ones."

Sanu shook my hand, too, and then everyone was hugging and clapping backs and smiling.

Surges of euphoria, relief, and disbelief swept over me, and my

heart swelled with gratitude and tenderness for all my fellow creatures — people and birds alike. In the midst of the merrymaking,
I just stood there, savoring it, observing the scene as if detached
from my own body. Through it all, the sleeping frogmouths seemed
oblivious. We studied them for a few minutes, then left them in
peace. Some of the birders said goodbye, but Harsha told me that
he had arranged an after-party at the house of nearby bird guru
Eldhose K. V., a well-respected, even-tempered character who had
spent many years studying the south Indian birds.

A few of us carpooled over there in a jovial, stately caravan. I was
invited in with a couple of other guests while a dozen other birders
stayed outside, watching the White-cheeked Barbets vie with Malabar Gray Hornbills on a fruit feeder in the yard. A table had been
set for tea in a small room. As I entered, things took an interesting
turn: a man dressed in a floor-length red robe rose from a chair.

"Greetings," he said, extending a hand.

"Noah, this is Kuriakose Mor Eusebius, a bishop from Kotha-
mangalam," Eldhose said, with elaborate politeness.

The bishop wore a dark beard, a tight-fitting cap, a high collar,
and a gigantic crucifix around his neck. He explained, in soft tones,
that he had driven quite a distance, and I couldn't help but wonder
what had brought such a distinguished guest to take tea with me.

"Are you a birder?" I asked, unsure what else to say.

"I have an interest in all living things," the bishop replied, "and
I heard about your world record. I predicted you would pass it this
afternoon, in spite of the rainy weather."

"Well, thank you for the blessing," I said, humbled by his words.

We sat down at the table with Harsha, Eldhose, and a reporter
who introduced herself as Preetu Nair. She quietly scribbled notes
in a small notebook while our little group sipped tea and chattered
about birds.

It was an oddly formal and starched way to celebrate a bird-watching record — nothing like what we do in over-the-top America — but why not? Over the next hour, as I enjoyed my tea, scarfed delicious tidbits, and fielded questions from Harsha, the bishop, and Preetu, my initial elation began to subside and deepen into a warm glow. As far as I was concerned, all was right with the world. We rejoined the other birders outside, and, many selfies later, everyone dispersed for the evening. Only then did I realize that it had been a very tiring day.

But it wasn't quite over yet: after dinner, I was fortunate to meet one more fascinating character, named Ben Mirin — perhaps the world's only birdsong beatboxer. Ben, younger than me, happened to be traveling in India on a grant from National Geographic to perform compositions of local bird songs through beatboxing, and he had been texting Harsha during his visit.

"It helps kids get interested in the birds around them," said Ben, who had scheduled shows at several schools in the area. "I record bird sounds in the wild, then use those audio clips to make beats that kids can relate to."

He did an enthusiastic demonstration, sounding less like a human being than a drum machine accompanied by bird sounds.

"I heard about your Big Year today from Harsha," he said, "and just thought I'd drop by. Congrats on the world record!"

As he said goodbye, I supposed that Ben's mission was about as wacky as my own. The world record had brought some interesting characters out of the woodwork.

The next morning, feeling slightly hung-over on excitement, Harsha and I stopped for breakfast at a street café in a rural town. As we entered, something caught my eye: a newspaper stand prominently displayed the day's headlines.

"Let's grab a paper," Harsha said.

On the front page of the *Times of India*, the world's largest English-language newspaper, my photograph was plastered underneath the headline, "Thattekad Birds Help Noah's Record Flight."

"That must have been the reporter at Eldhose's house," I said. "I didn't realize she was from the *Times of India*!"

The short story, with a special quote from the bishop, offered a straightforward account: "A reluctant smile dawned on the face of ornithologist Noah Strycker . . . Drenched in heavy rain and watched only by local bird watchers, [he] had set the world record for spotting [the] maximum number of birds [in] a year."

It was official, then. India — so crazy for records — proclaimed a new world record.

14

Hit and Miss

ON THE AFTERNOON of October 10, meteorologists noticed a disturbed area of low pressure over the remote Enewetak Atoll, which lies between Micronesia and the Marshall Islands in the Pacific Ocean. The next day, as denser air rushed in, weather forecasters in Japan upgraded the disturbance to a tropical depression, and on October 12 the system intensified into a tropical storm. When it tracked west toward the Philippines, the storm was christened Lando, and by October 17 it had graduated into a full-fledged super cyclone, equivalent to a Category 4 hurricane, with winds exceeding 150 miles per hour and a glaring, twenty-five-mile-wide eye visible on satellite images. Lando bore down on the Philippine island of Luzon, where more than 50 million people dreaded its landfall.

As the super typhoon blew toward the Philippines, I was perched seven hundred miles to the north, in the mountains of central Taiwan, with Wayne Hsu, the Director of Conservation and International Affairs at Taiwan's Chinese Wild Bird

Federation. After a long and productive day of birding, Wayne and I sat in a hotel room, examining Lando's updated forecasts on my laptop.

"You're going to the Philippines tomorrow, right?" Wayne asked.

"Yes," I said, "almost exactly where that typhoon is headed, to Luzon Island."

"It's supposed to hit tomorrow," Wayne said. "They're projecting several feet of rain and sustained winds over a hundred miles per hour when it reaches land."

"And my plane is scheduled to arrive there a couple of hours later," I added.

I felt more interest than stress about this development. If typhoon Lando slammed into Manila tomorrow, its impact on my travel plans would be trivial compared to the chaos for those who lived there. Besides, worrying about it wouldn't help, and I had more immediate concerns — like how to squeeze out a few last birds during my waning hours in Taiwan.

At that moment, my species list stood at 4,854 birds, fewer than 150 shy of my goal. For almost ten months, I had imagined the moment when I would hit 5,000: what it might feel like to reach such an ambitious milestone, and how relaxing to know that nothing could take it away. I had even, at the suggestion of a friend, considered getting the 5,000th bird tattooed somewhere on my body. The breakneck pace had not let up since setting the world record in India, and I now found myself within striking distance of the big 5K. Perhaps I could pass it in the Philippines next week, if I ever got there. Meanwhile, I had Taiwanese birds to snag.

To that end, Wayne spread out a map of northern Taiwan. We had just spent two days with Wayne's friend Kuan-Chieh "Chuck" Hung and a bunch of local birders who were tracking my Big Year through eBird. Word was definitely out by now about my adventure, and increasingly on my travels I encountered groups of birders, rather than just one or two. For me, these meetings never got old. It was energizing to share the world's amazing array of bird life with local people who knew their birds and their patches well. Everybody pitched in to find as many of Taiwan's twenty-six endemic bird species as possible during my short visit. We'd scored nearly all of them, including two fancy mountain pheasants — the Swinhoe's, which is electric blue, purple, and white with a long tail; and the Mikado, which is the country's national bird, depicted on the thousand-dollar bill and known in Taiwanese as the "Emperor of the Mist." We'd also seen the endemic Taiwan Blue-Magpie, an elegant creature dressed in blue, red, and black with an exquisitely long tail, flying against a cliff in the Dasyueshan Forest after a spectacular, misty sunrise. Now, with just a few possible birds remaining, Wayne and I tried to figure out a logical route.

"Here's where we are, in the mountains of north-central Taiwan," Wayne began, gesturing at the map. "And your flight to the Philippines tomorrow, if it takes off, will depart from Taipei, on the northern tip of the country. But the only endemic bird you haven't seen yet is the Styan's Bulbul, which lives down south, so to find one we would need to make a long drive, then catch a domestic flight to Taipei for your international connection."

"I suppose that's possible, but it's a lot for one bird," I said, "especially for a bulbul that looks basically like other bulbuls I've already seen in Asia. Is there another option?"

"Well, ye-e-es," Wayne said, as he uncapped a pen. "I've been thinking about it, and I believe I have a plan."

He spent the next few minutes drawing dotted lines, precisely annotated with times and places, until the map resembled the schematics for a sophisticated heist. The new route sacrificed the bulbul, but we'd have a chance to encounter a much more charismatic celebrity if all went well. By the time we turned in for bed that evening, I looked forward to an eventful day on the morrow.

October had been rewarding so far. After leaving India, I continued east, first to the country of Myanmar — formerly called Burma — where local birder Gideon Dun spent a week showing me some of the area's less-traveled sites. In Myanmar, "less-traveled" really means something: the nation was essentially off-limits to foreigners from 1962 to 2011 during an oppressive military dictatorship, and only recently began opening up. Along with his brother, Moses, Gideon is a former hunter who played in a rock band before taking up birdwatching. Gideon and I rode his motorbike through the mountains, prowled for birds around the breathtaking thousand-year-old temples of Bagan — one of the world's best-kept archeological sites — and waited out a flash flood after thunderstorms ripped through the hills one evening. Myanmar produced birds, but it gave the added impression of an expedition into the unknown.

From there, I moved to an entirely different environment in the Sichuan province of south-central China, where Sid Francis, a British expat obsessed with Eurasian birds and Chinese culture, hosted a wild road trip through frosted peaks, high ridges, and pristine river valleys. Sid and I topped out near 15,000 feet at Balang Shan Pass, admiring Golden Bush-Robins and Giant Laughingthrushes in two inches of fresh snow while prayer flags flapped and fluttered in a light breeze. By the end of the week, I came away with 215 species of birds and a new appreciation for China's natural riches — not something you generally read about in headlines.

I'd originally planned to fly straight from China to the Philippines, but a chance encounter in South Africa earlier in July inspired me to squeeze in this quick visit to Taiwan. In South Africa I'd stayed a couple of days in Cape Town with Callan Cohen, a full-time guide who one evening invited a friend to dine with us. That friend turned out to be Adam Welz, a campaign director for the anti-poaching organization WildAid, who knew Wayne Hsu, partly because Wayne had worked with Greenpeace in Asia. I was instantly persuaded to visit Taiwan — and now, three months later, here I was.

Wayne got us up early on my last day in Taiwan. We met a group of birders at the mouth of the Bazhang River, on the southwest coast, where we intended to scan for shorebirds before moving north on a tight schedule. A couple of minutes after arriving, though, Wayne suddenly started shouting something about a whale.

"It's on the beach!" he said. "Right at the mouth of the river!"

"A whale on the beach?" I replied, in confusion.

"Yeah, just aim your scope at that black thing," Wayne said, gesticulating. "You can see the flippers and tail sticking up."

Sure enough, I focused on the unmistakable silhouette of an enormous whale carcass on the sand about a mile away. It lay on its back, a dark shape with one pectoral fin jutting in the air, well and truly beached.

"Huh," Wayne said. "This must be the same sperm whale that washed up two days ago, a few miles north of here. The Taiwanese coast guard towed it out to sea to get rid of the carcass, but I guess it floated back to shore."

He snapped a photograph to post on Facebook, and within a few minutes a local news site had picked up the story.

"Look, my picture is in the paper!" said Wayne, showing us the grainy image under a Taiwanese headline on his phone's screen.

"Hey, wasn't there an incident with an exploding whale carcass in Taiwan a few years ago?" I asked, recalling a dim memory.

"Oh yeah," Wayne said, "A big male sperm whale washed up near Tainan — it was fifty tons, the largest whale ever recorded in Taiwan — and died on the beach before anyone could save it."

He told me the story ended badly after researchers, hoping to do a post-mortem, loaded the carcass on a flatbed truck and transported it through the city. A buildup of decomposition gases caused the carcass to explode, showering people and cars in blood and guts. Which maybe explained why this time the coast guard had tried to tow the carcass out to sea.

Wayne and I put the whale business behind us, said goodbye to the other birders, and hurried into Tainan just in time to catch a train — and not just any train.

"We could fly to Taipei," Wayne explained, "but it's faster to go by rail."

I'd never taken a bullet train before, so it was exciting to board this futuristic-looking high-speed rail. My last experience on a train, in India, had been on a cramped sleeper car out of Delhi, which ran like a polluted cattle cart. By comparison, this one felt like a sleek jet plane on rails, if not a rocket ship: inside, it was designed exactly like a commercial airliner, with an aerodynamic exterior contoured like a fuselage.

Once beyond the city limits, the bullet train glided along its track with a soft hum, picking up momentum almost imperceptibly. On a straight stretch, I used the GPS on my iPhone to gauge our speed.

"Holy cow," I exclaimed. "We are going a hundred and eighty-eight miles per hour!"

"Yeah," said Wayne, with a wry smile. "That's why the train is faster than dealing with airports."

His phone rang, and he had a quick conversation in Mandarin while I watched the scenery fly past in a colorful blur. Wayne told me, with obvious relief, that a birder he knew would meet us in Taipei.

It took us just an hour and a half to reach Taipei, nearly two hundred miles to the north, where Wayne and I stepped off the bullet train to find Hunter, a kind man who had volunteered to spend his Sunday afternoon with us, waiting with his car. The three of us drove out of the city but didn't get very far. On the outskirts of Taipei, on the shoulder of a busy highway surrounded by suburbs, we stopped to pay homage to a unique celebrity.

Wayne filled in the details. Nearly a year earlier, in January 2015, a young Siberian Crane had appeared briefly on Pengjia Islet off the north end of Taiwan, having drifted off course during its migration. This bird caused a stir in the birding community — the Siberian Crane is a critically endangered species with a global population of just 3,000 individuals, most of which migrate each year from Russia to eastern China, and it was the first time one had been seen in Taiwan. Pengjia Islet is under military control and cannot be visited by ordinary citizens, but the crane didn't stay there long. Incredibly, three days later, it was spotted again in a farmer's field outside of Taipei, within a short radius of several million people.

Pretty soon, the "little white crane," as it came to be known by the Taiwanese, was splashed all over the news. Thousands of curious people turned out to see it. The crane usually stayed in one particular field alongside a well-trafficked road, where it found a good supply of food, and it didn't seem to mind onlookers. When it dodged attacks from a stray dog and a passing hawk, local government officials feared for the bird's safety; they recognized this graceful crane as an ambassador of goodwill toward Taiwanese–Siberian relations, and so they assigned it a full-time security guard. Someone installed a webcam to let people watch from home, and a Facebook page with 13,000 fans posted updates. When members of a film crew inadvertently flushed the bird while filming in the area for an unrelated TV drama, they were duly fined for environmental disturbance, and schoolchildren formed a human chain to keep people at a safe distance. Volunteer observers began logging the crane's daily activities, hoping to figure out how to help it rejoin

its flock. In the first couple of months, this one crane had an estimated 60,000 visitors.

Now, nearly a year later, the bird showed no signs of leaving, and it had become a bustling local attraction. When Wayne,
Hunter, and I arrived, we found several dozen photographers
stalking the bird next to a souvenir stand selling crane-themed
knickknacks. Bright yellow signs in Mandarin and English warned
"Caution! Drive Slow: Crane Crossing." The crane itself took no
notice; it paced around its favored field with the slow elegance of a
ballet dancer, occasionally bending down to grab a morsel with its
serrated bill.

The bird stood a stately five feet tall, entirely white except for
a maroon-red face, pink legs, delicate black wingtips, and yellow
eyes.

"It has lost the colors of youth," Wayne said.

When the crane first arrived it was in juvenile plumage, less
than one year old, with rusty feathers over most of its body. Now it
was completely snow white like an adult.

Siberian Cranes can live to be eighty, if all goes well. But this
bird might not have a home to return to. Almost all Siberian Cranes
winter along the Yangtze River in China, and their preferred wet-
lands were recently destroyed by construction of the Three Gorges
Dam, the world's largest and most notorious hydropower project.
That dam was an environmental catastrophe in many ways, and
wild Siberian Cranes might eventually go extinct because of it. In a
way, this crane was lucky to be here.

We watched for half an hour while the bird steadily paced back
and forth, shadowed for a while by a friendly Little Egret. Did it
miss the company of family and mates? I watched the bird's yellow eye through my spotting scope, but its expression remained
enigmatic.

Then, remembering Lando, I checked my phone. To my surprise, my redeye flight to Manila had been confirmed.

"It looks like I'm flying straight into a typhoon tonight," I said.

"Guess we should get going, then," Wayne said. "But I'm glad you had a chance to see this crane — it is the most famous bird in Taiwan!"

With one last, lingering look at the crane, we stepped into Hunter's car and headed to the airport.

As it happened, that Siberian Crane stayed near Taipei for another few months. In May 2016, a year and a half after it had arrived, observers noticed the young crane becoming visibly restless. It made several short flights around the north coast of Taiwan, at one point taking shelter in a Taipei subway station while satellite news trucks broadcast its movements on local TV. Then, one day, it disappeared. Nobody knows whether it managed to rejoin its flock in China, or went to Siberia, or simply flew out to sea, searching for companions, unsure which direction to fly but compelled onward by the overpowering, universal instinct to return home.

Super typhoon Lando swung north at the last minute to make landfall about ninety miles north of Manila, hammering northern Luzon Island with sustained 115-mile-per-hour winds and torrential rain. Nine million people lost power, more than a hundred thousand took refuge in evacuation shelters, tens of thousands of homes were damaged or destroyed, and forty-eight people were killed. One city reported 51.9 inches of rain in twenty-four hours — more than four feet.

In Manila, warnings remained at Signal 2 throughout the typhoon, predicting only that "some coconut trees may be tilted" and "many banana plants may be downed." So, while the worst of the storm raged to the north, my plane lit on the runway of Manila Ninoy Aquino International Airport on a blustery, wet morning. It was unsettling to think of the chaos so close by, yet so far away. My most stressful moment came when an attendant, citing stingy carry-on restrictions, forced me to check my backpack, from which I had not been separated all year; I actually kissed it upon being reunited in Manila.

Despite the typhoon, Nicky Icarangal, a veteran Filipino ornithologist, was ready and waiting, to my great relief. Nicky had planned an action-packed week for us — four islands in seven days — but, as our first stop was supposed to be northern Luzon Island, which was now being pummeled by wind and rain, that itinerary was blown away. Nicky shook my hand and marched us over to the domestic terminal. In a few minutes, he explained, we'd take off toward the southern Philippines, where we'd be out of Lando's grip. Nicky had arranged for us to visit Mindanao, the country's second-largest island after Luzon, to search for the rare, endangered, and spectacular Great Philippine Eagle.

Nicky presented a stocky, trim, and tidy figure with dark, close-cropped hair and a patch of stubble on the tip of his chin. He wore hiking boots, a long-sleeved field shirt tucked firmly into khakis, and a watch tightly fitted to his right wrist, and he carried a duffel bag along with a mysterious hard, black, plastic case. He seemed to know everyone in the little domestic terminal, moving effortlessly through crowds at the check-in desks and nodding to acknowledge each acquaintance.

After checking his duffel, Nicky stopped at another counter, in a quiet corner of the airport, to hand over the plastic case.

"My toy," he said, a bit mysteriously, by way of explanation.

I was already dreaming of what the next days might bring. The Philippine Eagle, by length the largest eagle in the world, tops the most-wanted list for every birder who visits the Philippines. It's often called the "monkey-eating" eagle for its propensity to prey on macaques, but this predator hunts just about anything; it has been known to take down pigs, dogs, and the occasional deer. The eagle stands more than three feet tall with a light belly and a loose, shaggy crest, and is most often observed soaring above the canopy of unbroken jungle. It is Asia's counterpart to the Harpy Eagle I'd seen in Brazil eight months before. Finding both species in the same year would be a real coup.

The Philippine Eagle is rarer than the Harpy, though; with only a few hundred individuals left in the wild, these raptors are critically endangered. They require large tracts of intact forest to survive — each breeding pair is estimated to defend a territory of at least fifty square miles — and, as logging has accelerated in recent years, the eagles have declined. Today they are found in only a few scattered areas, with their last stronghold in the mountain forests of Mindanao Island.

Nicky and I were headed into the heart of that territory. I was amped to see an eagle, but also slightly concerned about what I might be getting myself into. During my Big Year, Mindanao was in the news for all the wrong reasons: armed guerrillas, militias, Islamic extremists, and outright criminals were active there, vying with each other in a messy and complicated resistance. The Philippine military, quietly backed by the United States, engaged in secretive operations to combat these groups, occasionally boiling into the international spotlight. At one point, CNN reported that 120,000 people had evacuated their homes to flee the fighting in Mindanao. This was nothing new — conflict has been ongoing since the 1970s in the southern Philippines — but it was worrying for a foreigner. Just four days before I arrived on Mindanao, the U.S. State Department issued a stern warning against nonessential travel to the region, citing a long list of terrorist incidents. "Exercise extreme caution," it read.

To see the Philippine Eagle, birders have traditionally visited Mount Kitanglad, an inactive 9,500-foot volcano in north-central Mindanao, but in February 2015 a group of birdwatchers got caught in the crossfire there, apparently between government special forces and the New People's Army, a communist rebel group. The birders managed to escape, but their guide was shot in the arm, and access to Mount Kitanglad had been dicey ever since.

To be on the safe side, Nicky decided we would try a different site, the Cinchona Forest Reserve, on the other side of the mountain's summit, where a pair of Philippine Eagles had recently nested.

"Don't worry," he said. "We will stay with a park guard who is friendly with the rebels, so they won't mess with us."

I tried not to dwell on the many recent kidnappings in the south Philippines, including a pair of Swiss and Dutch birders who were abducted on the nearby island of Tawi-Tawi in 2012. The Swiss man escaped in 2014 during a shootout, but the Dutch birder was still being held captive, more than three years later. The U.S. State Department had listed at least fifteen separate kidnappings during the first nine months of my Big Year, including four tourists abducted from a Mindanao resort a couple of weeks before I arrived. One of them, a Canadian, was beheaded several months later after a failed ransom effort.

We landed in Davao City, the bustling metropolitan center of Mindanao, in bright sunshine. Nicky picked up his luggage, then walked to a counter near the airport exit, where a uniformed man handed him the black plastic case. With precise, practiced movements, Nicky opened the case, took out a handgun, loaded it, and tucked the weapon under his waistband.

"Okay, let's go!" he said.

Mindanao offers a birder's paradise, not just for the eagle but for a host of other endemic species such as the Mindanao Bleeding-heart, a reclusive forest dove that looks like it's been stabbed in the chest, and the Black-and-cinnamon Fantail, a charismatic little songbird that sounds like a squeeze toy. Of nearly two hundred birds endemic to the Philippines, more than one hundred can be seen on Mindanao, and about fifty are restricted to this island and its outliers, making this area one of the world's richest for endemism. My skin prickled to get into it.

After driving for a couple of hours into Mindanao's rugged interior, we stopped along a muddy road where a house in a state of disrepair stood alone in a small clearing. I assumed the building had been abandoned until Nicky announced brightly, "Welcome to the Cinchona Forest Reserve headquarters!" Two men emerged to greet our arrival, and I was soon introduced to Emiliano "Blackie" Lumiston, the park's guard and caretaker, and his son, Ramil. Emiliano wore camouflage, sported a crewcut dyed blazing pumpkin orange, and smoked while we talked. He didn't speak English, so Nicky translated.

"Blackie is part of the Kitanglad Guard Volunteers," Nicky explained. "It's an indigenous organization that patrols the forest, helping protect this area against intrusions. Mount Kitanglad was declared a protected area in 2000, but it's under pressure from illegal logging and exploitation. The KGV has stopped a lot of development here in recent years."

Emiliano smiled warmly when I shook his hand.

"I'm glad to hear it," I said. "The birds need all the help they can get!"

"For the indigenous people, Kitanglad is a sacred site," Nicky said. "They know this place better than anyone. Even though they are poor, they are the forest's best protectors."

As a full-time guard, Emiliano was also an expert on the Philippine Eagle, my most-wanted bird in these parts. He told us that the local pair of eagles had finished nesting a couple of months before, but they were still hanging around. Our best chance would be to watch the skies from a nearby overlook where the birds could often be seen soaring over the forest canopy.

The four of us — Emiliano, Ramil, Nicky, and I — mounted two motorbikes to climb a narrow dirt track that no car could follow. Several miles above the headquarters, we reached a spot with a magnificent view: from a bare hilltop, the forest spread out like a flowing green carpet, with tendrils of mist swirling above it. Emiliano made a sweeping gesture toward the landscape under our feet, and Nicky said, "We will wait here all afternoon, if necessary. The eagles like to fly over this valley."

I checked my watch. It was just before noon, which meant we had about seven hours of daylight. With patience and luck, sometime before dusk I'd have an eagle in my sights.

We cheerfully settled into our vigil. Each of us remained mostly silent, lost in our own thoughts, while we continuously scanned the horizon. My mind drifted as an hour passed, then two hours, and I found myself daydreaming about the end of my journey. After ten months on the road, I was nearing the home stretch, but somehow I wasn't quite ready to be done.

And I wasn't even sure where, exactly, I'd be for New Year's Eve. For months now I had nurtured a secret plan, hatched with a couple of South African birders, to attempt to beat the world Big Day record on December 31 — to try to see more than 350 species of birds in a single day, more than anyone had ever recorded in one twenty-four-hour period. As a grand finale to my Big Year, setting two world records at once would be pretty epic, and we thought it might be possible in South Africa — especially with the help of a friend's private jet to cover the territory. I could fly from Australia to South Africa on December 30, meet the team, and go hard until the New Year.

But in early October, another crew of birders in Ecuador stunned the birding world with an announcement: after weeks of careful scouting, they completed a Big Day across the Andes and recorded 431 species of birds in twenty-four hours, smashing the existing single-day record.

"It's like beating the world marathon record by an hour!" enthused one of their team.

The South Africans were so impressed that they gave up — even with the jet, it wouldn't be possible to surpass the Ecuador tally in South Africa, which has fewer birds — and so, reluctantly, I canceled my New Year's Eve plans with them. I'd have to finish the year elsewhere.

"Hey, Noah, do you see that bird?" asked Nicky, and I snapped out of my reverie.

He was pointing downslope, toward a distant ridge. When I scanned with my binoculars, I quickly picked up what he'd spotted: a speck was rising slowly over the canopy, like a piece of dust floating in a lazy air current.

"Got it," I said, not quite sure what I had got.

All four of us immediately locked on. The bird was far away, at least a mile or two from our position, soaring against a backlit sky. I couldn't even see it with my naked eye, and the binoculars didn't help much. It was clearly a raptor, but which species? Nicky and Emiliano held an animated discussion.

"We think it's an eagle," Nicky said, finally, "but it's so far away that we're only ninety percent sure. Unfortunately, Emiliano says that it's in an inaccessible area, so we can't take the motorbikes any closer. Maybe it will fly over here for a better view."

The bird soared in broad circles, giving tantalizing looks as it banked in the thermals. I could make out its flat profile, bulky structure, and powerful flight, but that was about it. After ten long minutes, I watched the speck descend and vanish behind the ridge.

"I'm confident that was a Philippine Eagle," Nicky said, "but it was a terrible view."

Emiliano spread his hands in a gesture of helplessness: he'd found the bird all right, but today it did not cooperate. We'd waited all afternoon for a circling speck.

The eagle did not reappear. When night eventually fell without another sighting, the four of us returned to the dilapidated house. I crawled into a sleeping bag on a floor of rotten wood and lay there in the dark, turning over the day's events in my mind, pondering what I'd seen at the overlook.

Nicky and Emiliano were probably correct: the distant silhouette was likely a Philippine Eagle. But it had been so far off that I couldn't catch its field marks, not even the overall brown-and-gray colors. I might never have another chance to observe this bird — by the time I could return to the Philippines, it might be extinct in the wild — and tomorrow we had to look for Mindanao's many other species, because I'd soon be moving on. My heart ached. I wished, as I had so often lately, for more time.

When I closed my eyes, I knew that I would always remember exactly how empty it felt, that day on Mindanao Island, not to see a Great Philippine Eagle.

+ — + — +

Next morning, Emiliano woke us before dawn. He wanted to show me the Philippine Eagle nest, even though it was no longer in use, which required a short hike through the forest. Nicky agreed — we'd have a chance for a few birds I wouldn't find anywhere else.

After a hasty breakfast, we set out on a faintly marked trail leading straight uphill. Emiliano's son, Ramil, went first, clearing the way with a machete, while Nicky and I hung back, listening for birds. Nicky had an impressive ear, identifying each unseen singer as we walked along, occasionally stopping to zero in on one.

"Hear that?" he said. "That's a Stripe-breasted Rhabdornis.